HANDS ON FOREVER
A story of life-changing moments

Lots of love

Zoe xx

Dedication

This book is dedicated to my wonderful children, Charles and Vicky; my brilliant grandchildren, Harry, Matthew, Toby and Hannah; David, my soul mate; my twin sister, Zandra; and my devoted clients and friends who have encouraged me to write this book all the way to the end.

I also want to say how indebted I am to my parents, Hugh and Muriel Hall, for providing me with such gifts of insight that have shaped and coloured my life. I shall love you forever.

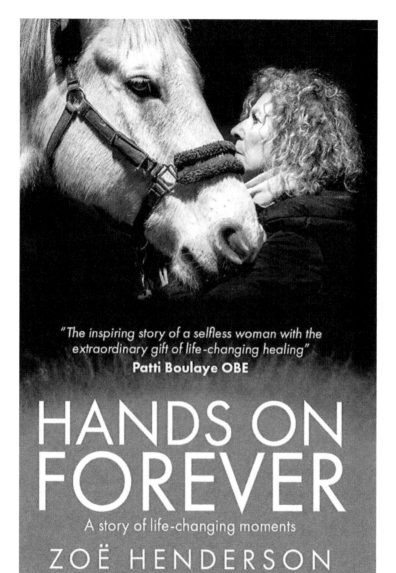

"The inspiring story of a selfless woman with the extraordinary gift of life-changing healing"
Patti Boulaye OBE

HANDS ON
FOREVER

A story of life-changing moments

ZOË HENDERSON

HANDS ON FOREVER
A story of life-changing moments

First published in 2017 by Panoma Press Ltd

This edition published in 2020 by Zoë Henderson

Cover design by Michael Inns
Artwork by Karen Gladwell
Photography by Emma Drabble

ISBN: 9798640423211

CONTENTS

	Testimonial	*vii*
	Client Feedback	*ix*
	Synopsis	*xv*
	Acknowledgements	*xvii*
CHAPTER ONE	Early years	1
CHAPTER TWO	Life as a teenager	13
CHAPTER THREE	My first job	25
CHAPTER FOUR	BOAC flying days	35
CHAPTER FIVE	Glentruim	45
CHAPTER SIX	Soul mates	51
CHAPTER SEVEN	Parallel friends	61
CHAPTER EIGHT	The islands of Bahrain	71
CHAPTER NINE	Sinking in quicksand	79
CHAPTER TEN	An Arab boy's dream	89
CHAPTER ELEVEN	Singapore	97
CHAPTER TWELVE	Say yes and do it anyway	107
CHAPTER THIRTEEN	Moissac, France	111
CHAPTER FOURTEEN	Returning home	117
CHAPTER FIFTEEN	Green of Angels	129
CHAPTER SIXTEEN	Emergencies	139
CHAPTER SEVENTEEN	Two people and a horse	149
CHAPTER EIGHTEEN	Fear and understanding	161
CHAPTER NINETEEN	Miracle baby	171
CHAPTER TWENTY	Horse whispering	177
	Finale	*181*
	About the author	*185*

TESTIMONIAL

I first had the good fortune of meeting Zoë many years ago at an event. There was something special about Zoë that drew me to her. She had a wonderfully calm and friendly aura. When we finally got together over lunch, Zoë mentioned things about my family and me that she had no way of knowing.

Hands On Forever is an inspiring story of a sincere, warm and selfless woman with the extraordinary gift, experience and knowledge of life-changing healing from an early age. Zoë is great at putting people at ease! What I find most appealing about her gift of healing is the way she puts it down to connecting with energy much more powerful than us—God's power.

My husband and I have had so much strength and support from Zoë's healing. After Zoë's first healing session with my husband Stephen, who was suffering from polymyalgia rheumatica, his pain diminished a great deal and Zoë told him why he was having what he described as bee-stings all around his body.

Recently, I collapsed with a severe case of dehydration after a full day's filming and a one-woman show in the evening. My entire body, from my feet to my neck, suffered the most painful cramps and spasms. I ended up spending 16 hours at the A&E

and the Acute Assessment Unit at the hospital. The next day, I went from the hospital straight to my book launch feeling very unwell and tired from lack of sleep.

I felt I had no energy left for my book launch let alone for another two hours on stage. Thank God, Zoë was there and selflessly went to work on me. She sat down beside me and put her hands around my midriff. The very deep and warm sensations from her hands gave me the energy to go on and perform that night.

Whether you are one of the lucky ones to benefit from Zoë's healing powers or not, I would highly recommend this book to you.

Patti Boulaye OBE
Author of *The Faith of a Child*

CLIENT FEEDBACK

Chronic back pain due to spinal curvature

"I came to Zoë after reading her book *Hands on Forever*, I have suffered with chronic back pain for many years having had two major operations for curvature of the spine and having exhausted all other forms of treatment and not wanting any further surgery. The pain I was experiencing was completely debilitating and making me feel old way before my time. To alleviate the pain, I was taking Tramadol three times a day. My surgeon had told me that when I move, I should imagine I am in a barrel therefore no bending and hardly being able to move at all. For me this was totally unacceptable as I am an active person who loves gardening, walking the dog and generally being active so I therefore had a struggle going on in my head as to what the expert said I should be doing and what I actually wanted to do and what gave me joy in my life.

"When I first met Zoë I immediately connected with her she is an extremely warm and kind person. After a few healing sessions, the pain had subsided considerably and I was able to reduce then completely stop taking the Tramadol. The pain has subsided considerably and I now have long periods when I am pain-free. I come back to Zoë for 'top-up' sessions usually when I have over done it! During the period of lockdown for the

Corona virus, the sessions are done over Facetime and although are at a distance, have the same results. I am so grateful for Zoë's healing, which has enabled me to enjoy my life.

Jane C, online healing sessions, April 2020

Easing cats with cancer

"Zoë's healing gift with animals has touched our lives deeply by helping our cats through difficult illnesses. Two of our cats were in the final stages of their illnesses when we reached out to Zoë, and through her healing and guidance they made a dramatic turnaround and came into much more ease.

"Our cat Baraka (meaning 'blessing' in Arabic) was in the final stage that cats reach when they are ill and lose all their life force and seek out a quiet place to rest and transition. Baraka had been diagnosed with kidney disease and despite doing everything we could with medical care, we assumed this was the decline into the final stage of the disease.

"Fortunately, Zoë was in Dubai at the time and she gave Baraka her hands-on healing. She also relayed to us that Baraka was feeling heat inside her body and that this is most likely a lingering bladder infection. Zoë gave Baraka a healing energy boost that helped her hold on, and we rushed her back to the vets who did indeed find an infection that they had assumed had previously cleared.

"After a long course of antibiotics, the infection fully cleared and Baraka has been back to her normal, bright, sweet self with no need for the extensive kidney support she'd been on before.

"As well as the healing Zoë gave Baraka at that critical time, her ability to communicate with animals helped to identify and locate the problem that had been missed by the vets and needed urgent medical intervention.

"We were also fortunate that Zoë was in Dubai when another one of our cats, Shams ('sun' in Arabic) who is in the final stages of a rare aggressive cancer, took a turn for the worse and we thought we were about to lose him. My husband and I were devastated to see him decline so quickly, first with losing his sight to the cancer, then with the cancer quickly spreading to his liver. We were advised that chemotherapy would be unlikely to improve the outcome of the disease, so we opted for caring for Shams and easing the final stage of his life as best we could.

"On the day he took a major turn for the worse, he lost what little life energy he had left, and seemed to be preparing to retreat for his final transition. A lump appeared on his throat that seemed to be making it difficult for him to breathe. Fortunately, Zoë was in Dubai at the time, and we hoped that her healing would help ease Shams's transition and passing. At this stage we were assuming the worst and could never have imagined what actually happened.

"Zoë gave Shams hands-on healing while he lay there with no energy within him, then slowly he started moving and turning to let Zoë's hands go to where the healing was needed. Zoë felt the lump in his throat and performed psychic surgery on it. I was astounded to then feel his throat and find that the lump had all but disappeared, with only a small trace left, and Shams could suddenly breathe with so much more ease.

"After 45 minutes of healing, Shams licked his lips, got up, and went off to find his food bowl and have a wander round the house. For the next days he continued to have his energy back and on the third day Zoë gave him a second healing. After this second healing, the lump in his throat completely disappeared.

Since then Shams has been going about his daily little joys of cuddles, eating, hearing the birds and smelling the breeze, and resting in between.

"Although Shams's cancer is too far progressed in the rest of his body to reverse, with God's grace, Zoë's healing has brought him more ease and life force which we believe has prolonged his life and significantly improved his wellbeing. Zoë has also reassured us through communicating with Shams that he's not in pain and that he's happy just being with us, as we are with him. We're grateful for every extra day and week we've been blessed with his loving presence, thanks to Zoë's healing."

Hala Mouneimne, Dubai, December 2019

Miraculous eyesight healing

"I met Zoë because my daughter had asked her to treat her and her horses. As I live not too far away I took the opportunity to ask Zoë for some treatment. I had nothing specific in mind as at my age (then aged in my 80s) various parts are wearing out, so I left it to her.

"I thought nothing more about it and about that time I had seen an eye specialist as one eye was cloudy. I was told that it was possible to treat, but without any guarantee. It involved injections of 'Lucentis' which is very expensive at £1000 a shot. I had to ask my insurance provider whether it would be covered, and if so, how much would they pay. The answer was they would cover me for £2000, sufficient for two injections. I arranged for the next consultation in the New Year as the Christmas holidays were approaching. When I went back in February, after my sessions with Zoë, the consultant examined me and simply said: "There is nothing to treat." I was dumbfounded and speechless. I simply could not believe it for a few moments. That was the moment I was convinced that the laying on of hands was a real miracle.

Bruce McKenzie, UK, November 2017

Polo pony with an infected hoof and flaking bone

"Zoë is an amazing miracle healer and I am so grateful to her and so is my pony Ballerina because she has saved her from surgery.

"Ballerina is my beautiful black Argentinian polo pony, age seven. About a month ago, she came back from the pasture with a wound on her rear left foot. It had a deep cut inside the sole. At first, the vet said it was not a serious matter and all what she needed was to stay at rest until it would heal by itself. Unfortunately, the vet was not a very good one. After three weeks, she was still limping and it was not looking good.

"I demanded the clinic send another vet. When that new vet came, after x-rays, his prognosis was very bad. A germ had attacked the bone, which had started flaking, and a spare bit of this flaking was dangerously loose in the foot. The vet urged me to have her taken into surgery at once. I was in a panic about it. This vet and his whole team at the vet clinic insisted that there was no other way, and it was urgent to do surgery before the foot worsened. I was in a middle of some dramatic issues with other horses and some other of my animals and I didn't feel comfortable about my mare going to their clinic. All the vets I asked for advice gave the same verdict.

"But I insisted on giving her a chance before going to the clinic for surgery so she was put under severe antibiotic treatments by injections directly in her leg plus others given by mouth. That is when Zoë appeared!

"Immediately, when Zoe came online to do the first healing on Ballerina, the energy levels went higher here. Even one of my cats, who had very bad bronchitis, was healed! And I also felt much better. Zoë started doing her miraculous first healing on Ballerina, and to the vet's surprise, Ballerina started doing better. Unfortunately, the Coronavirus confinement started then and Zoë couldn't come to my stables in France. Nevertheless, the healing sessions were held on Skype and it worked! The vets x-rayed Ballerina every few days and gave me just one week of postponing surgery but not more... amazingly though, each x-ray in those days showed Ballerina's foot was getting better and better. At first, it was only a little hope but then they acknowledged that the spare bit of loose flake was fading away. After just the second Zoë healing session on Ballerina, the vet said the spare bit of bone flake had gone (after new examination with x-rays) and that Ballerina would NOT need surgery!

"What an amazing and extraordinary healer Zoë is! I can't thank her enough. I will keep up healing sessions with her. Zoë is an incredible and wonderful angel healer."

Judith Belisha, France, April 2020.

SYNOPSIS

This is a story about how one person, from childhood to the present day, has used her natural awareness of the power of the energies that surround us, to help and heal her fellow man as well as all other living creatures that come her way.

It is an account of a carefree and happy childhood in Perthshire, Scotland where she was raised by parents who used their gifts of healing in the local community that became an innate part of her life from a very young age. Her father was a doctor and her mother organised his practice along with a very hectic social life that opened up a world of many characters to her and her twin sister.

There are extraordinary occasions related to the healing of animals from Edinburgh Zoo, from the nearby beach, from the side of the road, along with many people who needed help.

The chapters cover her life that take her to a career flying with BOAC, to marriage and children, to living on other continents and back to England that now acts as a base for her work and travels to near and distant places. At every stage, her healing power strengthens as she learns different disciplines in which to use it.

Her relationship with the angels and her face to face meeting with her own guardian angel are essential to her work and are an inevitable extension of herself and her success that benefit others.

Her stories of how she works, and the effects of her work, transcend comprehension but nevertheless are totally inspiring as she makes them sound so completely natural and part of everyday life. The matter of fact way in which she reaches out to the energies around her emphasise that they are there for all to use.

This is a continuing story of a life brimming with positivity and possibilities and one that is an illuminating example of how great one can be and what a difference one person can make when recognising and embracing her role on this Earth.

ACKNOWLEDGEMENTS

It really was the inquisitiveness of my clients and friends who wanted to know how I began this amazing adventure of my life. It was their insistent encouragement that gave me the impetus to put my fingers on the keyboard to which I have a natural adversity. I thank you all.

And of course, I have a huge gratitude to my children, Charles and Vicky, who have always been supporters of my work and to David, my husband, whose career also took me to the Middle East and Singapore where I developed my skills.

Isabel Contreras was the catalyst for the beginning of my work in Switzerland. She literally took me on board 'on a whim', through our extraordinary meeting that day in her office in Geneva. Isabel gave me the opportunity to further my work on my incredible journey into 'the healing world'. Thank you Isabel, and to Rony and Veronique Man of the International Academy of Healing for having me with them in Geneva to complement my treatments with theirs. Ann Starkey and Sue Powell also gave me enormous help and support with organising my schedules in Geneva over a long period of time.

My visits to Switzerland are enhanced by the kindness, hospitality and support of Jill Randle whom I have stayed with for many years and will never forget as we have known each other since before we were married. Many thanks to her and to Betty Billson who is always there for me whenever I need help. I also want to thank Jill Mackechnie and Marie-Regine Carty, who have hosted me in their homes, for their kindness and assistance.

In Nyon, Nicole Gubler hosts me in her home with enormous generosity as well as arranging my schedules for humans and animals. And I must acknowledge Liz Rollinson, my horse agent in Switzerland for several years, who has tirelessly driven me around to the sick horses and dogs without complaint.

In Wales, I'm very grateful to Katherine Harberd who acts as my horse agent there using her impeccable organisation for the horse events and horse and rider workshops and, not to forget, her amazing hospitality for having me to stay in her home.

My longstanding friend from my years in Bahrain, Susan Furness, now hosts me in her home in Dubai and manages every aspect of my visits there. I can't thank her enough as well as Maggie Williams who organises my schedules and assists me with my workshops and talks.

And I must thank Mahinda Mallawaarachchi, for his dedication, hard work and flexibility throughout my visits there.

As we know, there are no coincidences! So meeting the international best-selling author Carol Talbot whilst in Dubai was at a time when the seed of writing this book was growing in my mind. Within a short time, she had introduced me to the publisher Mindy Gibbins-Klein who encouraged me to write down my story and has patiently coached me to the very last page. Thank you both.

Finally, I must thank my dear friend from Bahrain days, journalist Jayne Beaumont, for using her professional skills to advise me and coordinate the pages of my book at the last minute and preventing a spiritual meltdown.

CHAPTER ONE

EARLY YEARS
Love and empathy everywhere

It was with his deep love of animals that Daddy inspired me to help the wounded. Little did I know that I would be following in the footsteps of his deeply caring nature throughout my life.

We lived in a little village called Stanley, near to Perth, in the heart of the countryside in Scotland and here he ran a practice with two other doctors. He was renowned by his patients for his kindness, compassion and tireless dedication to their needs, whether it be for medical attention or just words of comfort.

Zandra and I are identical twins. When we arrived, to the joy of our parents, two appeared at once! Mummy, through the earlier years of her marriage, suffered from having four miscarriages. She just couldn't hold her babies. About a year before our arrival and at the age of 40, in despair and with a last hope, she went to church and lit a candle. She silently wept as she sat in the pew and prayed to God and the angels for a child. A year later she had us. When we were told this later in our lives, she said we were the result of a miracle!

Daddy was devoted to us both and Mummy also in a different way. Mummy was an amazing PA for Daddy and she was on a 'social' mission of collecting Daddy's friends and patients for her well-known cocktail parties! She also worked for the Red Cross and was devoted to her work there. So, she multi-tasked between the two!

She loved people, reveled in the social whirl of her life and as far as Zandra and I can remember, never sat down! On the go the whole time, organising work or play. I certainly took on many of her traits so my genetic inheritance I owe in equal measure to each of my parents!

Zandra and I were always known as the Hall twins as no one could ever tell the difference to be able to identify 'ourselves'. We were inseparable as children and never got tired of each other's company. This strong bond has remained with us all the way through our lives.

In the forties, doctors had the responsibility of their own patients so that meant Daddy was permanently on duty. Many a time he was called out to a patient in the 'wee hours' of the night and he never had any hesitation in replying to them, "On my way," then got out of bed, dressed and left immediately.

Sometimes the journey to the houses, farms or cottages would take him ages, driving for miles through country lanes, dirt tracks and badly surfaced roads. In addition, over the winter season the treacherous routes were packed with ice or snow drifts and he had to battle through heavy snowstorms or torrential rain.

Once he arrived at his destination, he was welcomed in like an old friend with smiles of appreciation from his patients. He never hurried. He took his time, attended to the sick family member, as well as chatted, listened and helped the family with their individual personal problems.

He certainly had the old-fashioned bedside manner. At the end of the visit there was always a gesture of hospitality from the family with, "A wee dram before you go, Doctor?" And the bottle of whisky would be brought out. I think the answer here was most likely to be in the affirmative!

His passion for animals was equal to the care he gave to humans. He could never pass any of them that were in need. He had a habit of stopping the car when out on visits to rescue those that were in distress.

Once parked up, he would take out his little black medical bag from the boot of the car and reach inside for whatever he needed. Whether it be a sheep, deer, cat, dog or bird he would make sure that it was OK before he left the scene of the accident. Sometimes he would just need to clean up a wound of a stunned rabbit that had been dazzled by car lights or maybe untangle a sheep from a barbed wire fence.

If at any time he found an animal that was badly injured and there was no hope, he would get out his set of a bottle of ether and a mask and put the poor creature to sleep and out of pain. All the time whilst administering whatever was needed, he would talk, reassure, soothe and stroke them. The animals with cuts that needed to be stitched, including the birds that had broken wings, he would pop them in the car to be taken home and splinted.

We had a large house with seven bedrooms. On the third level, at the top of the house, there was a vast area that spanned across the building. This was our 'animal hospital' for the wounded to rest, be fed and healed back to health. We rescued many injured birds, of all kinds, mostly with broken wings. Daddy would splint them up and then they would have the freedom of the 'animal hospital' to relax with no fear of predators, sensing they were safe and being looked after.

When their wings were mended, Zandra and I helped them to find the confidence in flying again. One of us would hold a cushion and the other, from the far end of the room, would throw the bird up. It would fly across the room and be caught on the soft cushion landing. By this time, they had become very tame and we would have them on our laps, stroking, talking and giving them healing energy to bring them into total recovery. Then it was time for freedom to soar into the sky! When that time arrived, we would go in the car with Daddy with the bird on one of our laps until we came to the middle of the countryside and the wide-open spaces.

With excitement for the bird but a little sadness for us in letting it go, we would get out of the car and launch the bird up into the air. Very often, with still some attachment to us, the bird would circle us from above, not quite wanting to leave. Then suddenly there would be a squawk of gratitude when off it soared as far as the eye could see. It was always a magical moment.

Through the years, the number of resident animals came to about 30 if we were able to spot correctly all the creatures running around the house at one count! Mummy bred Chihuahuas and very often she found it too difficult to let the puppies go. She also showed them at Crufts quite successfully but she mainly went for the fun and talking to other doggie people rather than the win!

Daddy's surgery was in the house and had its own entrance so as not to disturb the family. The patients were greeted by many creatures, thus taking their minds off their complaints and keeping them amused. There were several tanks containing tropical fish as well as two baby alligators and several small

A story of life-changing moments

snakes. this was in addition to a wandering chimpanzee that was friendly but loved to lark around!

The chimpanzee habitually perched himself above the door of the entrance to the consulting room and when a patient came in, he would jump down on to his or her shoulders and grab their hair! Some patients laughed at it but others didn't. The regular patients became familiar with what was going to happen so could avoid the pounce!

As Daddy had a good friend who ran Edinburgh Zoo, throughout our many visits we would often end up taking home an animal in need of help. Of course, the alligators that came to be healed would become big and quite dangerous before they were returned to the zoo.

The snakes managed to slither out of their tanks, shed their skins around the house and end up in unexpected places like on the floor by the loo, in our beds, hanging from door knobs or lurking around a chair that you were about to sit on!

In the kitchen, we had a parrot that Daddy inherited from a patient. It was a noisy bird and screeched the whole time. Occasionally she would fall off her perch and land on the floor. If no one could be seen, she would waddle around in search of us. If she heard voices from behind a closed door, she would peck at it until she was let in to be beside the family!

One day when on a seaside trip, not too far away, we came across an injured seal stranded on the beach. It was a case of Daddy saying, "Come on Zoë and Zandra, let's get the rug from the back of the car and get the seal back home." Well, easier said than done. We laid the rug on the beach, rolled the seal on to it, then each of us took corners to hammock her back to the car. No, of course we couldn't put her in the back seat, wouldn't fit! So, we lifted her into the boot of the car and fixed the lid of the boot open with a long bandage so she could get some air.

On arriving home, decisions had to be made as to where we should put her. Finally, we thought that the most sensible place was the maids' bathroom on the ground floor, near to the back door. We excitedly filled up the bath with water and then lifted her into it gently. She looked perfectly happy and wallowed in the luxury. Ruth, one of our nannies, looked on with anxious eyes obviously wondering if she had to share this bathroom! No need to worry, she used our bathroom upstairs!

Through the daytime, we carried the seal into the garden to rest in nature. There we stroked her for as long as we could and keeping positive that she would get better. After a couple of weeks of tender loving care, she totally recovered and we were able to return her to the sea. Watching her swimming out rhythmically over the waves in all her glory was magical.

The numerous dogs and cats in our household would have their feeding bowls scattered all around, tipped up, empty or full. Yup, you needed ear plugs at times and maybe a clothes peg on your nose!

We were about four years old when Daddy and Mummy went on a cruise to the Orkneys whilst Daddy was working on board as the ship's doctor. We were at home being looked after by our nannies, one for each of us, who were part of our family and actually stayed with us until we were in our late teens. On our parents' return, to our surprise and great excitement, they had brought back with them a Shetland pony for us called Zeta. This was the beginning of my passion for horses. We kept her in a nearby field belonging to one of the local farmers and I spent many hours there learning to ride.

Who said that Shetlands were the best ponies to start on? More often than not, the 'Thelwell' breed are stubborn, have a mind of their own and go like the wind in the direction that they want to go, which was usually home for sugar lumps and carrots! However, I have to say Zeta had a gentle nature and didn't have many of the Shetland traits.

Mummy and Daddy were generous with their kindness, compassion and offer of help to all and loved people from all walks of life. With Mummy, her dogs were her passion and she always described them to us as 'fairies in dogs clothing'! She was also very intuitive and sensitive to the energies around her. She often talked about the angels performing miracles for us and through time, she said, we would see many of them ourselves.

She always said that we were never alone and we were being looked after, whether it be by God, the angels or a relation that had moved on who was watching over us. She also told us about white feathers appearing in front of us in random places, which were signs from our angels that they were listening to our prayers and were with us giving the help that we needed. She told us that butterflies also represented angels. Butterflies were a passion of Daddy's. He knew many species and had an extensive knowledge of them all.

From a very early age, I started talking to my angels and asking them for help, particularly when trying to heal the animals. We were certainly getting speedy recoveries with all our injured creatures and I could feel it happening as I was working with them.

When one of the Chihuahua puppies had problems with his ears, Mummy had taken him to the vets and he was given antibiotics. The pain and itchiness continued and after another visit it still persisted. Mummy was really upset and worried when she talked to me about him. "Don't worry Mummy, I will heal him through the help of my angels. He will be fine," I said.

Well this was the first time that I had said it out loud. Buttons was a gorgeous little puppy and had great big brown eyes, like saucers, let alone buttons! I took him in my arms and sat on a chair in the peace of the drawing room and he settled down on my lap. Not really knowing what I was doing, I just knew that something good would happen.

I asked for help from my angels and placed my hands over his ears and kept them there for about half an hour. roughout that time, I felt the heat coming through the palms of my hands and Buttons was getting sleepy. All the time I was asking for the healing to take place. Gradually his eyes closed and he was fast asleep. After some time, I took him into the kitchen where Mummy was feeding the other dogs. I passed him to her and said that he was fine now. Mummy thanked me with a beaming smile and the look in her eyes was that of surprise along with a glint of 'just knowing'.

Sure enough, from that day on, all symptoms had disappeared. Buttons was then my dog and was always at my side. I thanked the angels. Sometime later, I painted his portrait whilst he sat for hours for me in devotion. I still have it to this day in memory of our close bond.

Mummy was always laughing and planning the next event. For as long as I can remember, the house was full of people coming in and going out – patients, friends and guests to dinners and dos. In the repeated conversations she had on the phone with friends we heard, "Do come, I am only having a few friends over." We always knew there would be loads of people filling the entire ground floor of the house. She thought nothing about having 20 or 30 guests at a time.

Our nannies/helpers would be in the kitchen constantly on the day of the event putting together different canapés and nibbles. During the party we participated by handing around dishes of assorted yummies, and when the party was in full swing, as identical twins and dressed alike, we would be shown off as a sort of double act and guessing game. "Which one is which? Let me guess. Oh no, I have got it wrong! Identical, yes, but the noses are different! You are Zoë, no it's Zandra, I don't know!" So, it went on until they were satisfied that they could identify the right twin. It was a wonder that we hadn't switched places by the end of the night – within ourselves I mean! However, little did we know that in later years that is exactly what did happen in a certain way.

Identical twins where we lived in the 1940s were rare so we were stared at a lot. Mummy loved it and all through the years until we left home, and for some time after, the local paparazzi would follow our lives with updates in the newspapers. Zandra and I hated always being pushed in front of the cameras. Our lives were all in print with photos, 'the Hall twins', with write-ups on the latest events of our lives.

Our home was in constant bedlam with dogs barking, cats meowing, parrots screaming, doorbell and telephone ringing, birds screeching and whooshing noises of animals running around in different directions at full speed under our feet. A children's paradise!

Wet floors, dubious smells, food bowls and toys scattered all over the house with the chiming, in unison, of the grandfather and grandmother clocks in practically every room. Daddy was a fanatic about his hobby of collecting clocks and made sure they were at the right time and the same time, always.

As far as our attire was concerned, Mummy insisted that we dressed alike all the way through our childhood. Do we have an identity crisis? Who am I? We could merge of course without any problem but when we went our separate ways later, then what?

When school days started, we went to the local school and then to a private prep school and after that we were launched into a convent with lovely nuns, and some not so lovely! Actually a few were quite scary, especially the Mother Superior who was the head of the school.

Zandra and I sat beside each other and played together, as usual inseparable. The convent was primarily a boarding school but some pupils were taken in as day boarders as we were. I enjoyed the arts and spent as much time as I could in the art room whilst my sister was more into the sciences. I daydreamed a lot and my sister studied seriously.

My passion came to fruition in our early teens when Daddy bought us both ponies. This was my dream come true. We could already ride so it was time for serious lessons to be able to take part in eventing. Our daily routine began in the stables every morning around 5am to feed the ponies, exercise them and get them back in time before getting ready for school.

Daddy had already bought a piece of land and the old village hall next to our house for the stables to be built. The hall was turned into a function venue for all our fancy-dress balls and parties that we had thereafter. The stables were quite close to the back door of our house so gave us access to our ponies in seconds.

We had joined the Pony Club and at every possible weekend we would take our ponies to gymkhanas and one-day events, driven in a trailer that Daddy would hitch on to the back of the car for the ponies.

Slowly, or even quickly, I lost all interest in school and spent as much time in the stables as I could talking to Tan and Kontiki. Tan was my pony and he was very fast with a mind of his own. He bucked and reared so much that no-one else could ride him. It wasn't long before I was the only one he would let on his back.

We had bonded immediately and had endless conversations together. He had traumas of being badly treated in his life before he came to me but slowly, he trusted me and listened to my words of encouragement. He also taught me many lessons of trust, love and respect. He knew what I was saying and doing when I was trying to heal him and bring back his confidence. We were glued to each other. Very often I would slip away and sit on the stable floor with him and we would chat and I would pat him for hours. So much for my homework! I would go back to school the next morning, prep not finished or even started! Little by little I would catch up, fall back, catch up just enough, and so it went on. No wonder I failed exams!

Zandra and I were the first identical twins the convent had ever had so it was quite a novelty for all the nuns. The usual guessing game took place, which one is which, until we were soon being referred to as 'the twins'. It was a very small school of around 40 pupils with only 10 of us attending as day boarders. Our home was fairly near to the school so we were able to have the privilege of living at home.

Zandra worked really hard and was aiming to get all her exams – Highers and Lowers in those days – to be able to go on to a nursing career in the Royal Infirmary of Edinburgh, which she succeeded to do.

So, how about me? My passion was horses and I wanted to help animals. I also enjoyed being with people and helping them too but I hadn't a clue what I wanted to do. When the time came to sit my exams, the Mother Superior called me into her office.

"Close the door and sit down," she said before proceeding to inform me that I couldn't take the exams as I would probably fail them and give the school a bad name! What! Then straight after, "Why can't you be like your sister?" "Because I am not my sister," I replied and ran out of her office slamming the door.

I was furious when Mummy collected us that afternoon and I told her what had happened to me. Mummy was brilliant and I have never forgotten it. She thought for a while then said, "You can do anything you want to do. Look at Winston Churchill, he never passed an exam in his life and look what he achieved. Don't worry, there is something you will be doing that will surprise everyone."

As Mummy's intuition was always spot on, I wondered what she saw in my future but that conversation was as far as it went. She laughed after that and said, "Zoë darling, you will be fine." Those words have stuck with me all my life and I have passed on that story to many. I believed in miracles then as now and just had a feeling that something special was going to happen. But what I didn't know.

"Animals show us what's missing in our lives, and how to love ourselves more completely and unconditionally."

- Trisha McCagh

A story of life-changing moments

CHAPTER TWO

LIFE AS A TEENAGER
Horses, hunt balls and being a twin

My world was turning into a horsey world. At every opportunity, I was out in the stables with Tan. My favourite thing was to ride bareback down to the river, which wasn't very far away. Galloping through the fields, trotting through the woods and jumping over any fallen tree trunks along the way! Being in nature was magical and Tan and I loved every minute of it.

From time to time we went to Pony Club camp, which was great fun. There were about 12 of us with our ponies staying in a yard, literally, all together. Our ponies would have a stable each and then the empty stables beside them would house us girls. Camp beds were put in for us and we brought our own sleeping bags, along with our necessary change of clothing for a week. Each day we would have lessons of jumping, dressage or cross-country, go on treks, enjoy gymkhana games and then back to the stables and clean tack. Meals were taken around a camp fire, or we would have sandwiches on the trot.

One particular time, on the last day of camp, we were all taken to the local village fair as a treat. When we arrived, we excitedly went off in pairs. The fair was magical with all the lights, music, laughter and screams of excitement from the passengers on fast rides. My friend and I circled the fairground to see which scary thing we could go on, when we spotted a ride that looked like two aeroplanes at each end of a long vertical pole.

We decided to give it a try, although it looked pretty frightening. The pole was swinging up in the air and when the aeroplane capsule reached the top, it turned upside down and then upright again before descending back to the ground. We queued for ages it seemed then finally got on. We were strapped in and ready to go when I had this funny feeling of fear. It wasn't the normal feeling of anticipation and excitement but a feeling of a warning that something bad was going to happen.

I heard a voice in my head saying to me that the safety belt was going to snap when we turned upside down at the top. As we were going up, I told my friend to hang on tight to the sides of the capsule and that was all I could say. When we got to the top and the plane turned upside down, our seat belts snapped. Even though we fell into the safety grid as it was still moving down, I just knew we would be OK.

As the plane turned upright again, we came hurtling down to the capsule seats, at the same time screaming to get someone to stop the ride. As the sides were open, we could have easily fallen out and been flung to the ground. My friend actually fell on top of me and we hung on to each other tightly until the ride was stopped and we got out.

People were mingling around us to see if we had been hurt but, amazingly, we got off unscathed. The ride of course was then shut down. Afterwards I just knew that we were being looked after. We were fine. This was one of my first experiences of divine intervention.

Mummy was always saying to us, "You will be fine," no matter what difficulties in any area of our lives we went through. She was always positive and encouraging. Keeping positive is the most important thing for all of us. No matter what! "I am fine," is a great affirmation to use, and it has certainly served me well throughout my life. Thank you Mummy.

Around this time, we were all noticing that Daddy was drinking too much. Mummy was sort of in denial of the fact that it was getting worse and tried to sweep it under the carpet.

Very often before we went to bed, Daddy had already retired and Mummy would ask me just to check in on him. They had separate bedrooms due to the fact that Daddy snored like a train, which often vibrated through the walls! I dreaded this but always did it if asked. This time when I went in, I saw Daddy lying in bed, no movement, no snoring, his eyes open and glazed. I was only around 13 years of age and why I did this I will never know. I thought he was dead but I didn't want to worry Mummy or Zandra until the morning.

I shouted out to Mummy, "He's fine," ran into bed, said goodnight to my sister who was in the bed beside me, covered my head with the blankets and cried silently all night, with the knowing that I would have to break the news to Mummy and Zandra in the morning. I was asleep when the bedroom door flew open and there was Daddy, with a happy face, saying, "Morning girls, time for school."

Through the years thereafter, I tried to help him so many times, getting distraught that I couldn't fix him. For years, I felt responsible to save him, and for years I didn't talk about it to anyone but family as I wanted to be loyal to him and not betray him. Mummy used to say that he was sick and couldn't help it. This indeed was the truth. Of course, the lesson here is that we can't hold up another person, and we can't fix it. We can help as much as we can but ultimately we are not responsible for other people's lives. We are only responsible for our own body, mind and soul.

More and more I spent time in the stables with Tan, or rode to our 'little piece of Heaven' down by the river. He was my best friend and confidant. I talked about everything, laughed and cried.

Now I was preparing myself to start art school, as Zandra was preparing to go into nursing, which was her vocation. For me, I still hadn't a clue! I loved painting, so followed Mummy's days at The Slade School of Fine Art by going to Duncan of Jordanstone College of Art in Dundee, which wasn't too long a journey from home. I did the general 1st year but really wasn't enjoying the work they were giving me, so gave up and just did my own creations by myself. For hours I would paint and create, which I found cathartic. I was in my own little world and I am sure the angels had a hand in it, by channelling guidance through the sweeps of my paintbrush.

One time, when we were having a family holiday in Spain, I had lent Tan to a friend of mine whilst we were away. Near the end of the holiday we had a call from her to say that Tan had been in a nasty accident and his leg was badly injured.

Panic welled up in me and we cut our holiday short and raced home. As soon as we arrived, we went straight over to my friend's yard. When I saw Tan, I was shocked and my heart sank. How were we going to save him? He was in a terrible state. We all looked at each other with pain and fear in our eyes, but I knew that he was so happy that I was now with him.

He was brought back to our stables and the vet had said there was really no hope, that he would have to be put down. Apparently, he had been attacked and beaten by thugs and chased over a steep drop. His leg was bad and he couldn't walk. I was devastated. I pleaded for the vet to sling him, to allow the mending to take place, but he said that it wouldn't help, and he was in too much pain.

Through the days before he had to go, I stayed with him and cuddled and patted him, and did all I could with talking to the angels, trying to heal him, but I couldn't do anything to save him. The loss of him broke my heart and left me with the guilt of not being able to do anything.

So later, when my sister's pony got sick, I was determined to bring her back to good health and felt positive that something could be done.

On his last visit, the vet had said that she was in a really bad way. She had grass sickness and severe laminitis. She was in a lot of pain and was finding it difficult to walk. She was 17 at that time, so she was quite old but was normally full of life and in high spirits. He said there was nothing else they could do.

It was around 5am when I ran out of the back door of the house to check on Kontiki. As I went into her stable to say good morning and have a chat, her sad eyes looked at me in despair. Oh no, she could hardly stand on her feet, she was wobbling all over the place and obviously in a lot of pain. I decided that I would stay with her as long as possible, and do some healing around her hooves. It was really a big ask I suppose, but nevertheless we weren't going to give up on her.

I crouched for ages, going from one leg to the other, around and under her hooves, keeping my hands on the parts that needed help, for as long as I could. Asking for help and talking to her all the time of course, saying that she would be fine. Then around her body and up to her head, to talk and soothe her and tell her how much we loved her.

I continued the same procedure every morning, and little by little she got better and better until she could walk and trot around the paddock. She was back to her normal self and full of life. She enjoyed every minute of her new lease of life until she eventually left us at the age of 20. The vet was amazed.

It wasn't until many years later did we realise what a privileged childhood we'd had. Our social life in our teens was quite extraordinary. As Daddy and Mummy had patients and friends in every circle, we were invited to all the social functions going. Endless cocktail parties, dinner parties and balls.

When we were 18 years old, one of the most prestigious events was the hunt ball. Actually, there were two in a row and Zandra and I used to attend them each year. We always knew many of the guests, from marquises and countesses, lords and ladies, to the rest of us, and the whole affair was spectacular.

We would prepare for these a couple of months ahead. The rules of tradition, manners and etiquette were strict and everything had to be perfect. We had our own party of invited guests, and first and foremost was to make sure that we knew all the dances well, especially the highland reels.

There were certain well-known clan chieftains who would hold dinner parties in their castles well ahead of the date, to check us out! Back to school? These soirées would include perfecting our dance routines before we set foot on the floor of the ballroom. However, most of us were born in the saddle, and born to dance, as we had lessons for each as soon as we could walk. So, we knew them already. Albeit, it was a bit nerve-wracking!

Table manners? Well, they were impeccable as the majority of the party were born with the proverbial silver spoons in their mouths. I remember thinking there's a lot of birthing going on

A story of life-changing moments

here, let me give birth to my perfect steps! I am not brilliant in dance coordination, so let's hope I pass, and not pass out!

So, it was practise, practise and get it right. It wasn't just the steps of the dance but the way you looked at your partner, turned your head and where you put your hands. Automatic after a while! However, the reels were fast and you had to keep in perfect timing. The ballroom had suspended flooring that thankfully gave with the up and down rhythm of the steps. But if you landed when the floor was coming up, it could hurt. And in the past, with the weight of a full dance floor, it had been known to break a leg!

Were we ready? Zandra and I had been forced to have an afternoon sleep as it promised to be a long night. We excitedly got ready in our white ball gowns, yup, they were the same, tiaras on top of our heads, and our tartan clan plaids across one shoulder. White gloves, shoes and handbags to match.

The most important thing to take with us was the traditional little white booking card, with all the ballroom dances and reels printed inside, and a gap beside them for your partner's name. From the top of the card hung a gold pencil, to wear out hopefully with a fully booked card! It was up to the men to approach the ladies and ask us for the pleasure of the dance. Then we would both decide whether we wanted a ballroom dance or a reel.

The men wore their dress kilt and jacket, and a skindoo, which is the ornate knife tucked into the side of their sock. For the second night, we ladies could wear any colour of long ball gown, with or without the tiara and sash. Before we got to the ball, we attended the pre-dinner party hosted at the same practice night venue. Here we would eat as little as politely possible as we knew we had a feast of a formal dinner followed by breakfast to come. At this point, we had a head start of filling our dance cards to ensure we had the dances we wanted with our own party.

We drove in convoy, which often took up to an hour as the castles and mansions of the majority of the hosts were in the middle of nowhere, set deep in the country. The bagpipes would be playing as we were arriving, and waiting at the bottom of the steps to pipe us all in.

Yes, it was something like a period film as you walked up the red-carpeted stairs to the venue. Chandeliers lit all around with amazing flower arrangements all over. Many flights of wide semi-circle stairs leading off to banquet rooms and other areas for lounging around in.

On the ground floor a large bar and reception area welcomed everyone in to mingle, chat and drink champagne, which then led to the wide-open double doors to the ballroom. The vast ballroom, which would probably hold around 200 people, had the perfect ambiance of glamour, with the delicate lighting of chandeliers and side lamps to fit the elegance of the tradition. The hunting horn would be blown, and we would be ready to celebrate the season.

The spectacular sight of all the ladies in white ball gowns with different tartan plaids was breathtaking, with all the tiaras sparkling along with the other jewels on necks, wrists and fingers. They were accompanied by the handsome men in kilts of every tartan, swishing away to the music of the night. The dance form followed alternating speeds, so there would be a Scottish reel, followed by a waltz, foxtrot, a quickstep or something slow.

All the men in the bar area were darting around, dance cards in hand, asking 'the pleasure' from the lady of choice, scribbling

A story of life-changing moments

the name down, arranging the place to meet for the dance, to finally dashing away and on to the next! Zandra and I had great fun swapping some of the partners on our cards, as no one knew the difference anyway, so we took our own choices of dance, rather than the men. OK, if there was one that we really liked, we wouldn't trade!

The dinner was a feast, and laid out in style, and you tried to get invited to sit beside your favourite guy there. There was also a night club at the top of the building, so you could be whisked away during the gaps in your card to go up for a jive, rock 'n roll or a Charleston.

The breakfast at 5am was a sobering up kedgeree or bacon and eggs. By that time our stilettos were killing us, so the assorted sizes from each of us ladies were pushed off under the table discreetly, in silence and relief. The ball always ended with 'God Save the Queen'. Shortly after the hunting horns were blown with the cue of 'your carriages await'. Then we all bid goodnight or rather good morning to fall into our transport, exhausted.

The parties were endless and often miles away, so we usually stayed the night, but numerous ones were at our home with Mummy being in her element. We were well known for our fancy-dress balls, which we held in the old hall that we had converted next to the stables. We hired a band and served a buffet supper. Our themes varied from 18th Century to a Tramps' Ball. Everyone honoured the stated dress code and was attired appropriately.

The best one we threw was our 21st birthday ball and, believe it or not, for our mother we decided to wear exactly the same dress and hairstyle, and promised each other that it would be the last time ever we dressed alike. The ball was formal, so Zandra and I wore long white ball gowns of a different style from the hunt balls, and to the fashion of the year, but equally stunning without the plaids and gloves. Our guests were in many colours and all the men were in kilts.

For this milestone event, we were given as a 21st birthday present the venue of one of Daddy's patients. It was a huge castle in the middle of the estate, with the grounds to fit a fairy tale. The long sweeping drive went on and on, and eventually arrived at the floodlit castle, surrounded by a moat.

When we alighted from our cars, we walked over the drawbridge to the sound of bagpipes, with the piper standing at the entrance of the massive oak doors leading into the castle. Walking down the long halls to the ballroom we passed many suits of armour, and the walls were adorned by family portraits, stags' heads and swords.

Champagne was served throughout the night, along with a buffet banquet. The band played a medley of reels as well as modern and we all danced into the small hours. The splendour of the ball and the atmosphere created, gave us the most amazing and memorable birthday present.

Throughout the ball, we thought we would really play on the 'twin' game for the last time and enjoy muddling everyone up. So we swapped places, partners and information to all! Even our parents got confused! It was then, through this evening, we discovered that we could look at each other at any time, at the same time, and know what we were thinking.

Not long after that evening, our feelings for each other's ailments and accidents got stronger. We realised that we already had the advantage of speaking to each other without opening our mouths. We could easily tune into each other, so this was

A story of life-changing moments

probably going to continue throughout our lives. Joined at the hip at a distance!

"Like every star in the Universe, like every tip of your finger, like every pattern of a snow flake, you are 'You-nique'. Cherish that gift."

- Kiran Shaikh

CHAPTER THREE

My FIRST JOB
Compassion and joy

It was time for me to think about what I was going to do in the way of work. Luckily, through no effort on my part, my father spoke to me one day about a friend of his who was the manager of a nearby hydro hotel, who was looking for a social organiser. Just up my street, I thought, mingling with lots of different people from all walks of life, children, games and functions. Sounds like fun, with a variation of duties, perfect!

Mummy of course was thrilled to bits with the idea, and had certainly trained me well in all social etiquettes and function preparing, for all occasions! With our excitement of the prospect, Daddy rang the manager and an interview was set.

On the day I set off to the hotel, I had so many questions in my head, like could I do it and did I really want it? Oh well, too late, I was on my way, driving along the country roads with my stomach churning, with waves of nerves. 'You can do it, you can do anything you want,' I heard Mummy's voice in my head.

The fact was I hadn't any training as such for this job, and obviously no exams needed as it was a recommendation, or maybe a favour for Daddy! In those days, folk were bartering for many things: a day on the shoot in which Daddy was part of the syndicate, some venison, a pair of grouse or maybe for some medical advice.

Anyway, there I was, sitting in the manager's office, definitely wishing I wasn't there by now! However, he was a really kind man and didn't ask me too many questions, but mainly told me about the duties that I had within my job. The only question he had was, "Do you think you can do it?"

"Absolutely," I answered, praying please angels help me to learn everything very quickly so it looks as if I know it all! We then looked around the hotel with the vast ballroom, dining room, card room, library, chapel, swimming pool, billiard room, etc. There were a couple of hundred bedrooms and then the staff bedrooms were either in the attics or in the basement. He showed me the bedroom that I would have in the basement, as I would be living in, due to the really awful hours I would be working. Oh no, do I really have to sleep in here I thought? Bars on the only window and very little light! However, I thought it wouldn't matter very much as it looked from my work schedule that I would only be there to crash and, at that, only for a few hours.

Yup, I was right, after the first week there I thought I was never going to have a full night's sleep ever again. It was coming up to high season and activities had to be prepared: golf, badminton and tennis tournaments, swimming galas, whist drives, treasure hunts and dances. Then every other week I did a rota of managing the dining room.

In actual fact, I really enjoyed it, as after everything was set up and organised, my duties were to wander around and chat to the guests, and make sure that everyone was happy. I spent many evenings with the elderly residents and they told me their life stories. We had around 40 of them who had booked themselves in long term. Many of them sat on their own and needed company, so I made sure that I did my rounds and tried to spend the same amount of time with each.

After a couple of years, and really in the swing of everything, I met a lady whom I got quite friendly with and she told me about her career as a stewardess with BOAC. It sounded amazing and I thought that's definitely for me, going around the world and being paid for it. Permanent holiday!

It was my last season at the hotel and I had grown friendly with a lot of the elderly residents, including Mr Ray, a retired vet. We used to spend many an hour in the conservatory, talking about animals and his experiences with them. On the evening of the opening of the season, it was tradition for me to choose a partner and invite him to commence the dance with me.

It had been a hectic day of preparation, making sure that all the events had been organised. I stuck the notices on the board, along with sheets to be filled in with the names of the participants for different matches and competitions. Then of course there was the speech that I had to prepare, welcoming the guests and giving them information on the programmes that were set for the week.

It was a formal do, of around 100 guests. All the ladies were in long evening dresses and the men mostly in kilts. The ages of our guests were from teenagers to the very old. The younger children and babies were tucked up in bed and monitored regularly by parents and helpers throughout the evening.

By this time, all had been done and I had decided that I would ask Mr Ray to honour me by being my partner for the first dance of the season. A lot of the regulars often hoped it would be them, and others dreaded being asked! It could be a bit intimidating as usually we would be the only couple on the dance floor for a while, until others gradually joined us.

Even though he was in his eighties I knew he loved ballroom dancing, and did it very well. Many a time I had seen him at these evenings, waltzing around the room with pride in his steps. This time I knew he would be delighted to be asked.

Well, where was he? He was usually in the conservatory, reading a book or chatting to the other residents. No, not there, so I thought he must be still in the dining room. Not much time before kick off!

Yes, I spotted him at his regular table and it looked as if he had just started his meal. Swiftly I approached him and asked him if he would like to partner me for the first dance of the season. He went positively pink with excitement and accepted profusely with lots of nodding his head and a thank you, yes please. Now he was going to bolt down his meal to get a seat near the stage and wait for me to come to him. Just a reminder to him before I left, "Don't forget your teeth, Mr Ray!" He had a habit of taking out his dentures and putting them in a glass of water on the table whilst eating his meal, and very often they would still be sitting there well after he had left.

The time for me had come to get on the stage, the band already up there had just done a drum roll to stop people talking, and a cue for me to join them. Oh well, here we go, I said to myself, I hope I have remembered everything, but most importantly, I hope Mr Ray has remembered his teeth!

I finished my speech of welcoming the guests and gave them information of several activities, then made my way across the room to where Mr Ray was sitting. Yup, great, a nice toothy smile from ear to ear! Dentures in! The band had started to play

A story of life-changing moments

a waltz – great, I thought, nice and slow, as I stretched out my hand to bring him to his feet to begin the dance.

As we were waltzing perfectly around the dance floor, he was getting redder and redder in the face and seemed to be getting a bit excited. Calm down, I thought, it's only a dance! Little by little more guests rolled in, then everyone waited and watched, like it seemed forever. Oh, hurry up and get up, I thought, my partner is getting flustered.

We had done a couple of circuits around the ballroom and still no one else got to their feet, when he said to me that he thought he would like to sit down. I felt that maybe he was a bit nervous, and yes, the dance floor was empty and everyone was looking at us. Ah great, here they come, one couple got on the dance floor, then fairly quickly others took to the floor.

I said to him, "You are doing fine, let's just do one more round and then I will take you to your seat." "Yes," he said and was actually loving every minute of it. Then the horrors began. It was like a sack of bricks when he slumped to the floor, still holding my hand. I went numb and froze with fear. It was one of those moments of disbelief, is this really happening?

In tears, I knelt down beside him, shouting out for someone to get the doctor. He was with us in minutes but Mr Ray was already dead. I was devastated, and in a way blamed myself for encouraging him to carry on dancing when he said he wanted to stop. His time had come and his soul had chosen to leave during a happy time.

We had a great friendship and enjoyed each other's stories of our passion for animals, and I will always cherish those memories.

We had our own mortuary in the hotel down in the basement as so many of the elderly residents came to us to remain here until the end of their lives, so it was a necessary room. The resident doctor confirmed that the death of my friend was instantaneous and there was nothing anybody could have done.

The next day, the hotel was a buzz of 'Chinese whispers' with everyone passing the news on to the next, with additions to the truth and exaggerations of the event.

It was really interesting the comments I got from the guests. The middle-aged people: "What an awful thing to happen for you." The teenagers, joking: "I hear you killed someone on the dance floor last night." The elderly residents: "What a way to go!" Yes, indeed, what a way to go! He danced all the way to Heaven.

Even though my sister and I were now separated by our careers, we both tuned into each other and very often felt each other's physical pain from a distance.

It was one particular night, when I had fallen asleep after a very busy day of organising and running events in the hotel, that I was awakened in the middle of the night with the feeling of a knife cutting through my tummy. I could hardly breathe with the pain.

My first thought was to get help, but I actually couldn't move to be able to ring the bell. I was stuck in this pain when, all of sudden, I just knew it was not me, it was my sister's pain. I waited and waited for it to subside, sending my sister positive vibes and asking my angels to help her. Once the pain had completely gone, I thought I would ring Mummy first thing in the morning to see if she knew what was happing with Zandra.

A story of life-changing moments

Sure enough, when I did ring, straight away Mummy said that Zandra had to undergo a peritonitis operation in the middle of the night, but she was fine. Relieved that she was OK, I said to Mummy, "When you speak to her, tell her that at least she had an anaesthetic. I didn't!"

We always know when there is something wrong with each other or when an accident has occurred. As children, if one of us had a sore tooth, or a tooth extracted, the other would have the same pain, at the same time. But the weirdest thing, which still happens to this day, is that when we are together for any length of time and then part our ways, we swap characters on departure. We say our goodbyes, in tears more often than not, and then that's it, we are in each other.

Although we look alike our characters are quite different. Many a time once we are settled back to our own places, we would ring each other and say, "Please will you get out of my body?" It is a strange feeling, I speak the way she speaks anyway, and we have the same mannerisms. However, we swap actions, she acts like me and vice versa. This can last for a couple of days or even up to one week, and we always get ourselves back at the same time. When my sister got married, I felt totally lost for a while, but then I realised that the bond we had for each other would never change, and it would be forever. Her husband was a lovely man and he adored her. We were very close and many of the happiest and fun times I had were with them.

It was one time when I had the weekend off, I went to stay with them but knew I had to leave on the Monday to get back to the hotel. Ava Gardner was in residence with her cast and they were shooting a film in our area. I had to be back before they went on set to make sure they had everything they needed, so an early start was called for.

It had been snowing non-stop throughout the weekend and on the Monday morning it was freezing and the roads had iced up.

It was around 5am and driving could be difficult as the roads hadn't been sanded as yet. I said my goodbyes to Zandra and Euan, with the last words from them, "Be careful, the driving conditions are appalling." "I will," I replied and off I went.

I was driving very slowly in my little Mini, as I knew it wasn't the best of cars in these treacherous conditions. It was around 5am, and yes, the roads were lethal. Horrors! I was skidding all over the place on these deserted country roads and beginning to think I should have turned back and abandoned my duties.

I started to go into a bend that had a deep drop at the edge of the verge and there was nothing I could do. I tried to control the skid, but impossible, and too late. My car skidded sideways and off the road, summersaulting over the 30-foot or so precipice.

As I was tumbling, rolling, upside down, over and over, from side to side, and being flung from the front seat to the back, my mind was all over the place. The noise was horrendous of breaking glass, crunching metal, and it just went on and on. The flying glass was circling me, with the car scrunching up and getting smaller and smaller.

The thoughts were going round in my head, praying to God and my angels to save me, and thinking this is meant to be the time that my life is flashing through my head. No, I had none of that, and I kept positive and just knew I would be fine. Finally, the car came to a halt and I thought now what? I was trapped inside.

Everything around me was like a crunched-up can of metal, no glass in the windows and the doors squashed in and jammed. I was calm and felt I was being looked after. One of my main thoughts was oh no, I am going to be late for work! How stupid is that! After sitting still for a while to gather my thoughts, I managed to climb through a window and sit on the ground for a moment to feel around my body and see where I was hurt.

Nowhere really, and no pain. I had a little piece of glass in my knee but that was all. Luckily, as it happened in those days, I wasn't wearing a seat belt, as the steering wheel had been pushed into the driving seat. In addition, I was wearing a fur coat, so was cushioned and protected from flying broken glass and metal.

Other thoughts I had in that roller coaster were: What is Daddy going to say when I tell him that I have crashed the car? And Mummy's words: 'Keep positive, you'll be fine.'

After I sat for a while, I thought I had better climb up the bank and try and get help. I scrambled up, passing bits of the car along the way, including my hand luggage. Finally, I got to the top and sat on the roadside waiting for someone to come. Not long after, a car stopped and a man got out.

It was Ava Gardner's chauffeur on the way to pick her up to go on set. "Zoë, what on earth are you doing here?" he said, as I pointed to the drop below. "I'm fine," I said, but of course he insisted on taking me to hospital for a check. Looking at the mess of the car, it was a miracle that I escaped alive.

I had my check in the hospital and everything was clear, so I went back to work and got on with my day. It was "divine intervention" for sure. I was saved by my angels. Not my time to go. I knew it, with that feeling of just knowing.

So, what next? I thought lessons to learn, embrace your mission. So, what's my life purpose and where am I going? Realise your dreams, visualise it and it will come about. Negativity will block your progress!

One dream had already come true, with constant dreaming, wishing and visualising my life with horses, to having them.

The next step I didn't know yet. Well I knew it, but I just didn't know I knew it! That would be at soul level. Helping people and animals, for sure, all those in need of help. Life is a journey of the unknown, with surprises and no coincidences along the way.

"It is good to have an end to journey toward; but it is the journey that matters, in the end."

- Ursula K Leguin

CHAPTER FOUR

BOAC FLYING DAYS
Overcoming fear and separation from my twin

Yes! It was time for my first interview with BOAC. In those 'old and golden days' there were two things that girls wanted to be and yearned for: an actress or an airline stewardess. Glamour on the stage or glamour in the skies? From all the stories I had heard from my friend in the hotel, the more I wanted to fly. She had been all over the world and had many amazing experiences and met all sorts of interesting people. The stopovers on trips could be a week at a time. The fun times and stories she told me were intriguing.

So off I went, driving from home to Glasgow with a threepenny bit tucked in my bra, which Mummy gave me for luck! "There you go darling, good luck, you'll be fine," she said. I was immaculately dressed for the part, felt confident, I looked OK with a dress and jacket to match in grey and a just below the knee skirt line, high heels and bag to match and of course, the compulsory gloves.

The journey was easy up until the outskirts of Glasgow when the traffic seemed to get a bit heavier, and then into slower traffic ahead. For no reason at all, the driver of the car in front of me jammed on his brakes and I went straight into him. Oh no, I thought, now I am going to be late and that is an absolute 'no no' for the company, never be late.

Out I got to speak to the driver of the car I bashed, and never mind all the apologies from either of us, but out came a rambling jumble from me, explaining that I was going to an interview with BOAC, the most prestigious airline in the world and difficult to get into, I must be on time and now I was going to be late and a feeling of panic set in.

He was absolutely fabulous, tried to calm me down, and said, "Don't worry, we will exchange phone numbers and sort it out later. Off you go and good luck!" Thanking him and near to tears, off I went. Of course, inevitably I was a little late, around 15 minutes, but even that really wouldn't have been acceptable. However, the member of staff that I met first listened to my story and then said, "On you go to the waiting room." There sat six girls, immaculately groomed, looking like models from magazine covers, all sitting with their hands in their laps holding a pair of gloves that were being screwed up and fiddled with, showing nerves of anticipation. We hardly spoke to each other but obviously we were all feeling the same.

I sat in silence, saying my prayers and talking to my angels to get me through this one. Should I succeed, there was a second interview in London. When I eventually got into the interview room, the guy was lovely and easy to talk to. The first thing he said was, "Are you OK? I heard you had a bump in the car on your way." I affirmed I was fine then felt at ease straight away. Then he asked me the usual question of why I wanted to be a stewardess.

My first answer was that I really enjoyed helping people and talking to people of all ages, kinds and race. Well sort of, but I bet all the interviewees said that. Then I thought my previous job was a real asset with all that experience it gave me. However, throughout he didn't give me a clue as to whether I was through or not, but the energy between us felt good.

I drove home happy and relieved that it was over. When I took my threepenny bit out from my bra, there was a bruise and imprint of it on my skin from hitting myself against the steering wheel with the impact of the shunt. Would that be a sign? I thought. Signed and sealed?

Yes! I was in and passed the first interview. The second in London was apparently quite gruelling. The scariest thing for me was taking the flight as I was petrified of flying! Whoops! I hadn't flown very much at all, a couple of flights to France and Spain for holidays and that was it.

Once on board, I settled myself down in my seat and hung on tight to the armrests, thinking any minute now we are going to plunge to the earth. Of course, I knew this wasn't going to happen but I felt the anxiety anyway. I didn't accept any refreshments from the stewardess when offered, in case I showed my fear. The worst was that I couldn't even look out of the window. How on earth am I going to do this for a living? I thought. Oh well, I will just need to feel the fear and do it anyway! I will be fine.

It was the same procedure with the second interview, but this time there was a panel of four people, firing questions at you. In addition, they handed you a cup of tea and watched how you walked to your chair with it and if you crossed your legs properly when you sat down, if your deportment was good and dress was appropriate. As if that wasn't nerve-wracking enough!

When I was finished, I looked at all the other girls waiting for their turn looking stunningly beautiful. I thought, yes, I am sure they fit outside, but what's on the inside? The saying at that time for the airline was 'if your face fits, you're in' and these girls were known as 'la crème de la crème'.

It seemed an eternity waiting for the letter from BOAC and finally it arrived. I ran upstairs to shut myself in my bedroom to open it with Mummy and Daddy waiting downstairs in anticipation. Oh my goodness, I was accepted. triumphantly, I flew downstairs to give them the news. Great excitement all round! Then it was the waiting game to prepare myself, pack up, and leave for London.

The airline had allocated me digs in Hounslow so I had no need to hunt around for accommodation. I had not long paid off the instalments for my tomato-red MG Midget, and was very excited to be able to drive it on that long journey to London. My new adventure was about to begin. How exciting and terrifying to boot!

The family that I was with were lovely, kind and encouraging. They had had many stewardesses through the times and so knew the signs of exam nerves, insecurities and homesickness.

The room I had was tiny with a small window. I got used to the planes flying over, but they were so low I thought they could easily be coming through the window, and the noise vibrated through the whole building. Anyway, I suppose it helped me to keep awake through the massive studying I had to do. This time it was nose to the grindstone, and I was determined to get good marks in my exams, get my wings and get flying!

The six weeks were pretty tough, including SEP training, jumping on to aircraft shoots and into the swimming pool, pulling each other on to rafts, saving each other, to crawling through smoke tunnels at top speed. The deportment classes were vital and we were trained by Lucie Clayton who had us walking more or less with books on our heads, sitting with legs crossed and gathering knowledge of pristine make-up and hairstyles. We all spoke the 'Queen's English', which was a must, and we were from similar backgrounds. And yes, some of them were snobs, but most were lovely. My trainer was very strict and a bit intimidating I found, but she wanted the best out of us, and for us.

Ultimately, that is what we got, and I was very grateful to her for the lessons she gave us. I will never forget her words of wisdom on many occasions. There was one statement that I will never forget, "If you have a steady boyfriend at home, keep him." Temptations in the skies, men that lie, Caribbean beaches, crew parties, passenger chat-ups? Yup, the mind boggles!

Yippee, got my wings, thank you angels, ready to fly with you! Soon after that, it was flat hunting. I found one pretty quickly in Wembley Park that had two stewardesses in it already. Sorted! Here we go!

We had three grades of stewardesses: A Bird, B Bird and C Bird. A Bird was working in First Class, B Bird economy and C Bird Supernumerary. We flew VC10s and 707s. I was on long haul, which meant the long trips with long stopovers. Our trips would vary in length; our longest would be three weeks, which often extended due to delays along the way.

The best was we would be flying to amazing islands like Fiji, Barbados, the Seychelles and more. Then the plane would leave us there for several days to a week before the next plane came in. Magic! By the time we came home from these trips the crew became very bonded. Some more than they should I noticed!

My first few flights were a bit nerve-wracking, especially as I still couldn't look out of the window! When a passenger ever pointed to places in view, like mountains, and asked me what they were, I would always answer, looking at them straight in the eye, "not quite sure, madam. I have not long been in the airline, I will just find out from one of my colleagues." Got away with that one! However, after a few flights I was fine and really enjoyed the breathtaking views of everything.

Our duties in the cabin were not only to serve food and drinks but to really look after the passengers. Talking to the nervous ones to comfort them, helping the mothers with their babies, looking after unaccompanied minors and any that were feeling ill. This we all took very seriously and we patrolled the cabin regularly through the night flights to make sure all was well. I loved the caring side to my work with all the different ages. Very often I would offer help to mothers with crying babies, give them their bottle, cuddle them and walk up and down the cabin to rock them to sleep. In fact, through my flying years I had a reputation with the crew of being able to take any baby, with whatever their problem, and get them to go to sleep.

I would walk up and down the cabin, patting and cuddling him or her on my shoulder, having taken it from a very tired and distraught mother. Yup, and humming a lullaby out of tune with the wrong words, they were asleep in no time. Believe it or not, my children and grandchildren inherited this tune, and guess what, it works like magic! Maybe it's the sleepy angels at work!

The unaccompanied minors were the children either going to or returning from boarding school, or being handed over to estranged parents. We handed out toys, colouring books and puzzles to amuse them throughout the sometimes very long flights. Occasional sweets and crisps to keep them happy between the main meals, sometimes stories and chats when they were sad. All the children were given little passport books to join the junior jet club; the magic event for them was to visit the cockpit to have their junior jet books signed by the captain and have a chat, and in addition be shown how the aeroplane was flown. It was wonderful seeing their little excited faces coming back down the aisle from their awesome experience.

The elderly passengers who were flying alone always needed a bit of TLC and chat about their families they were visiting or the purpose of their flight or just a chitter chatter! Sometimes they were very nervous, so I would sit beside them, hold their hand and comfort them. Although we were always very busy with food and drinks service, it was during the night that some passengers needed extra care. In fact, we did regular patrol strolls through the cabin to make sure they were all OK.

After flying for a while, I took the First Class training and was soon to be promoted to being an A Bird, and was very excited. This meant that I would be promoted to First Class soon after. The First Class service was literally first class. We did silver service with silver cutlery, teapots, flowing champagne, roast dinners carved in front of the passengers served on silver platters from the trolley, plus desserts to die for. Three or four courses with all the trimmings, to equal the top well-known restaurants anywhere.

I was just about to go on my last trip as a B girl, so I rang my sister to say that I was off, and good luck. She was expecting her first baby and the birth was due in a few days. I promised her that when I returned, I would come straight to Scotland to see her and the new baby.

It was a really busy flight 'walking' to New York, and I knew most of the cabin crew, which was great, and felt the anticipation of a good fun trip. When we got moments of a break, we would stand in the galley grabbing a quick bite, chatting and laughing and planning our off time for when we got to our destination, starting with a crew party in one of our rooms.

"Right," I said to the steward whilst finishing the last mouthful of a sandwich, "better get the meal service started." I began to pile the meal trays along my left arm ready to hand them out. It was a balancing act sometimes, when you tried to carry more than you should for speed, in getting the passengers fed as quickly as possible!

As I was going down the aisle and passing the first few trays out, I suddenly had the most terrible pains in my stomach. Oh this is not good, I thought, and the pains came in waves and got worse. Suddenly I was doubled up and dropped the remaining trays, which were quite a few. How embarrassing was that! Starters, main dishes, puddings, cups and all and sundry went flying down the aisle, not to mention meat, veg, puddings, cups, and cutlery flying on to the laps of many.

Whew! The steward was at my side and scooped me up and half carried me into the galley, whilst another crew member cleared the debris. I was sitting on the floor in the galley clutching my stomach thinking what on earth is going on, when I got the message.

"Are you OK?" the steward asked. Yup, typical, here we go, I thought, I am going to be taken off the plane in a white jacket! "Yes, I am fine, don't worry, I am in labour, it will stop soon!" I said. "What?" he said. "No, no it's not me," I replied, "it's my twin sister's pain, she's in labour." Then all of a sudden it stopped. I looked at the time on my watch so that I could verify the time of the birth of her little girl.

When we eventually got into the hotel that night, straight away I made the call to my brother-in-law to congratulate both of them on the birth of their little girl. Our times matched! This time, we both felt the pain!

"The guardian angels of life sometimes fly so high as to be beyond our sight, but they are always looking down upon us."

- Jean Paul Richter

CHAPTER FIVE

GLENTRUIM
A handful of white feathers

Zandra and her husband Euan had now moved and were ensconced in Euan's ancestral home. Here he took over the title of Laird, and Zandra, Lady Glentruim. The castle was situated in 'a little piece of Heaven' not far from Inverness, overlooking amazing views of roaming hills, woodlands and rivers. Here I spent many wonderful times, in-between my flying trips. And yes, the castle was haunted!

When they entertained, they entertained in style. The castle offered an ambience of faded elegance. Ancestral guns, swords, portraits, paintings of shooting and hunting scenes embraced the walls of every room. The dining room was large, and set out to dine in style, silver candelabras lined along the middle of the long inviting table. Silver pheasants placed around the incidental tables, stags' heads on the walls glaring down at you when having your feast. Many a tale was woven in this dining room!

The drawing room was set for entertaining guests, with French double doors opening out to sweeping semi-circle staircases going down to the vast front lawns of scattered colours of rhododendrons, assorted trees canvassed by spectacular views.

When guests arrived for dinner, we would have cocktails and canapés here. Then, as tradition, the men would put an arm out to their lady of choice to escort into the dining room, to then sit beside her.

The family's personal bagpiper would be standing ready, in his kilt, to pipe us all in to our feast. All the men would be in formal kilts and jackets and the ladies in long evening gowns. Even when it came to friends coming for dinner, we would all still dress up for the occasion, but minus the piper!

The smoking room had a leathery look, with scattered sofas all around, a large open fireplace, which was always burning, even in summer, as the central heating was non-existent and we were always frozen. I was forever standing with my back to it, as close as I could with my skirts pulled up to get the heat charged through my bones! The walls were heavily shelved with books of all sorts: hunting, shooting, fishing and clan history.

Stale cigar smells wafted in and out, along with the log-burning fire. This was the room that the gentlemen retired to after dinner to smoke their cigars and drink brandy, usually reminiscing of game hunting stories, when the ladies would go into the drawing room in front of the vast open log fire to talk about the men!

Then there was the boudoir, our chilling-out room. Smaller in comparison to the rest, with a conservatory attached, where we could sit in the summer with a view of the long winding drive and woodlands of trees. This was the family room where we spent most of the time when we were on our own. A cosy room with the compulsory open log fire, where I stood, as usual, in my elegant pose!

The numerous bedrooms had four-poster beds, antique dressing tables and heirlooms, along with the necessary china chamber

A story of life-changing moments

pots in situ, should one get caught short in the middle of the night to race down the corridors to the loo, or the fear of running into a wandering ghost or two! It was normal to hear the marching of soldiers from time to time, or have the feeling of 'who was that?' or 'what was that?'

The top floor was for the staff and the corridors up there were certainly creepy, along with the turret room on the second floor, which had a definite feeling of a presence. Here the rumour was that an ancestor that had lived here had thrown herself from the window of the turret to her death. I know when I slept there, I always slept with one eye open and the other one shut! One night, I was woken up with a cold hand holding my hand. Needless to say, I closed both eyes tightly and drew my hand away!

I became used to seeing and hearing 'things that went bump in the night' and definitely here we all caught a glimpse of a wandering lady from time to time along the corridors.

I was getting really excited about this trip to Glentruim as I had a whole week and was looking forward to having quality time with my sister. Euan was away on a fishing trip with his friends and we would have the whole time to ourselves to chill out.

The A9 can be a tedious journey when the traffic is bad but this time there was very little on the road so the drive was a joy. The countryside was a canvas of autumn colours. The leaves on the trees in their glorious shades of orange and amber, the fields of white and purple heather scattered across the hills, was indeed an artist's dream. It was a beautiful sunny day for a drive in the highlands.

As I was motoring along and not far from Glentruim, I spotted, in the layby ahead, a fluttering white bird of quite some size. What on earth is that? I thought, and slowed down to be able to identify the creature and decided to pull in. Oh my goodness, it was a chicken! The poor wee thing was fluttering and looked as if she had been stunned.

Remembering my childhood with Daddy and how he would stop the car to care for an injured bird, I had no option but to do the same. How did it get there? It must have been flung out from a chicken lorry on the way to a not very good ending. Well, we would change that.

I got out of the car and went over to the white chicken. Her eyes were closed tight and she was then unconscious. Occasionally she would twitch, there were no signs of cuts or breaks but she definitely was in a bad way. I picked her up gently, there was no movement but her heart was still beating. I put her on the passenger seat in my car and drove off in haste to Glentruim.

When I arrived, Zandra greeted me at the front door with excitement. I quickly told her about the chicken, which I then carried into the house. We decided to take her into the boudoir and see what we could do for her. I sat on a chair and put her on my lap and stroked her continuously, giving her healing and keeping positive that she would be OK.

We made a little bed for her and put her in it whilst I was unpacking and settling in. The rest of the evening we sat together with her on my lap, hands on her, chatting, eating, along with the occasional glass of wine!

When bedtime came, she was still unconscious but we snuggled her up in a bed of straw in an open cardboard box and left her for the night. The next morning when we came down, she was still asleep but twitchier, so I put her on my lap and did the same as the night before. Suddenly she opened her eyes and was as bright as a button. She had the most amazing red eyes I'd ever seen.

A story of life-changing moments

She looked at us but didn't seem at all frightened. She jumped off my lap and just walked calmly around the room then waddled back to me. The whole time during my stay at Glentruim she never left my side and followed me everywhere. Even when we went for walks, she came with us.

When I did eventually leave, Zandra decided that she would keep her as a pet, and from then on, Whitie, our handful of white feathers, became a member of the family and followed Zandra everywhere. I wondered if she could tell the difference between us. A handful of white feathers or maybe a handful of angels!

My next trip was within a couple of days, so back to my flights and back to work, or was it work? I thoroughly enjoyed my time with BOAC. Each time I saw a roster in the post I would be excited to read the details of my next adventure. I was given a Moscow visa and very often went there. It was a weird feeling roaming around the streets as you always felt you were being followed. In the hotel there was what we called a 'dragon lady' posted outside the lifts on each floor of our rooms. She spied on us and was meant to make sure that there were not numbers of people going into our rooms. We were sure the rooms were bugged in case they discovered some sort of conspiracy going on! It was an uneasy feeling. However, the city was magnificent and we enjoyed the sights.

On that route, we went to Anchorage, which was amazing. Often the temperature went down to -30° and we could actually see the sea with frozen waves in perfect form. Of course, we had to be well wrapped up in hoods, gloves and our faces covered to prevent frostbite.

There were certain pubs we went to that were underground. It was like being in hidden igloos. The food we ate, especially the fish, was spectacular and very often we would take some back with us on the plane – Alaskan crabs in boxes of dry ice to be enjoyed when we got home along with caviar and a bottle of champagne!

One eventful but disturbing time, we were on a trip to Beirut when there was an attack there and I have to say that was quite scary. We were told to stay in our hotel and keep away from the chaos in the streets. We could hear the gun fire and see fires from our windows and men with guns running through the smoke and devastation.

We were constantly ringing our families to say we were OK and it obviously sounded worse at their end from what they were seeing on the television. Our plane was delayed coming back due to the fighting and therefore our extended stay of just over a week was worrying to our families at home. It was certainly a relief to be home.

My flying years with BOAC were some of my best years and it was a privilege to be one of the 'crème de la crème' of the 'golden age' of passenger jets.

"If we all could see the world through the eyes of a child, we would see the magic in everything!"

- Chee Vai Tang

CHAPTER SIX

SOUL MATES

David and the children at Moy Lodge

It was strange, but a comfortable feeling that I was going out with the boy next door, so to speak. David's parents were best friends of my parents, and Daddy was their doctor. We lived in the same village and grew up together, and actually, we were born in the same nursing home. There's history for you!

After he left university, he got his Private Pilot's Licence before joining the RAF. During this period, he visited me in London many times and then fortunately, he was posted not too far away. Our relationship soon changed from being like brother and sister and sharing many secrets together to getting engaged.

It was a bit of a shock to our parents, as it almost felt like incest as our families were so close. However, it was certainly a blessing as our parents didn't have to worry about finding out the backgrounds of each of us, such as, 'What does your father do?', a classic, or 'What are your intentions?', another. It was obligatory then for David to formally ask for my hand in marriage from my father when the time came.

When eventually we got married, our first home was a 'buck and ben' as they say in Scotland! One bedroom upstairs, living room and kitchen all in one downstairs. We were in the middle of the Yorkshire moors just outside Haworth, in Bronte Country.

We lived in a small community of cottages and here our neighbours were like family. There was nothing but hills, dales and sheep around us. At this time, I got close to my neighbours and the wives helped each other in every way. David was now flying with North East and I was still in BOAC, commuting to Heathrow for my trips.

When I was pregnant with my first child, I gave up flying. The cottage was really too tiny for children so to begin with Charles slept in a carry cot at the side of our bed until he progressed to a cot on the landing.

It wasn't long afterwards we moved to Ilkley to an enormous house with huge grounds, with apple trees, landscaped gardens and a tennis court. We were just below the Cow and Calf and the views of the Dales were to die for.

Shortly after Vicky was born, David joined British Airways so we were on the move again. Right, time for house hunting and I knew exactly what I wanted so I decided to drive to London with the children for the adventure of the search! Well, it was not as easy as that, as the kids were only 20 months apart and Vicky was still breastfeeding. Anyway, off we went on the long journey, with occasional stops to feed my children and a nappy change. I was staying with a friend in Surrey whilst I was hunting, so that was easy.

It felt like 100 houses I had viewed, and the children clearly were getting a bit fed up with this game. So, after a week I decided that I would give us just one more day and then enough was enough. Home was beckoning!

A story of life-changing moments

I was about to give up, when I was sitting in the estate agents in West Byfleet, with baby in arms and toddler by my side, flipping madly through endless papers of houses for sale when I spotted just the one.

"That's it," I said to the man behind the desk, passing the information sheet to him. "Oh sorry," he replied, "this house has just come off the market, today in fact." "Well ring them up and say that I am very keen." "Not possible," he said. "Anything's possible," I replied. "Lady Cole is adamant that it is off the market," he continued, but through determination and not moving from my seat, with two wriggly, noisy children by this time, he dubiously rang her and we had a viewing straight away.

I drove to the location via Old Avenue in West Byfleet, a beautiful avenue of trees of all colours and sizes, then turned into a long driveway to the house, which gave me the feeling of excitement and 'I'm home'. I just knew this was it before I even stepped in the door. Charles was getting restless now and, oh no, Vicky had pooed all through her Babygro and was definitely in need of a bath!

Lady Cole opened the door to us and gave us such a warm welcome. I introduced ourselves and straight away I said, "This is it; we will buy it." "What?" she said, "You haven't even seen round it." "It's OK," I replied, "I just know it, I know it is the right home for us."

She looked at the children and saw that Vicky was in distress. "She needs a bath and a feed," I said. "No problem," Lady Cole replied, "let's go upstairs and give her a bath and a change of clothes, then you can feed her." Brilliant, I thought, I am home, and as we followed her upstairs, I skimmed the house with a look here and there along the way. It was just right. Not even faded elegance, but a spacious friendly worn-out look!

We bathed Vicky and then went downstairs and chatted in the drawing room whilst I breastfed her, with Charles at my side.

In the time it took to feed an infant, all was agreed through our conversation, and we set off for a tour of the house.

The entrance hall was a room large enough for entertaining, leading off to the drawing room of average size, with an open fireplace. Separate dining room, large enough to hold eight or more for dinner, and French windows leading out to a front patio, overlooking a perfect garden of around three quarters of an acre, with a sweet little Wendy house in the corner. Perfect for the children and totally secluded. Whoops, what was that I could see at the end of the garden? A railway track hidden away? Oh, David won't like that if it is noisy!

The kitchen was also large with a laundry room leading to the back door. At the side of the laundry room was a walk-in larder. Masses of storage for all kinds of foods, tins, bottles, and jams maybe, if I ever had the inclination to make them! No, maybe not, boxes of chocolates then!

There were three floors with four bedrooms on the first floor and two bedrooms and a storage or office room on the top floor. All the rooms needed a lick of paint and that was all, I thought. A bit old-fashioned, but I liked that, and oodles of character.

When we had toured around a couple of times, we sat and had a cup of tea, whilst Vicky slept and Charles played on the floor with some of his toys that we had brought with us. Through our chat, I could hear the trains at the bottom of the garden and, to me, they sounded quite frequent, so I asked Lady Cole if she was bothered with the noise of the trains. "Pardon?" she said, so I repeated, and then had to speak louder. "No, not at all, I never hear them," she said. Oh, she's a bit deaf, I thought, or maybe a bit more than a bit!

For a while when we did move in, it was, "Those bloody trains, I can't live with this," from David, until slowly by slowly we got used them. Actually, it didn't bother me a bit, I found it quite soporific and no, I am not a bit deaf, on the contrary, my hearing is very acute, I can hear every soft sound and more.

Intuitively I felt there was more than met the eye in the energies of the house and I had asked Lady Cole if there were ghosts. She said that she had never heard any. Hmmm.

We had quite a bit of furniture but not enough really for all the rooms. A lot of the furniture we brought from our house in Yorkshire and the rest I collected in antique sales, auctions, second-hand shops and anywhere I could find period stuff. I loved the 'oldie worldie' things, and little by little I furnished our home.

We did a cosmetic job to fit the ambience of a kind of faded elegance! The house was built on King Henry VIII's route where he would travel in his coach, drawn by horses, from Woking to London, so the terrain had its own history. I could imagine the countryside in those days with the still remaining old oak trees scattered around the avenues and gardens. What stories of times gone by they must nurture within them!

Very often on my furniture hunts I would spot something just right, like a walnut wardrobe or chest of drawers, and I always wanted it home right now and couldn't wait to order a delivery van.

The routine I had was to scour the parked vans or empty lorries on the roads nearby my find. Then, if there was a driver in the vehicle, I would approach him and say, "Would you like to earn a quick tenner?" Then I would have to say very quickly after that statement, "To take a piece of furniture in your van to my house about a mile away."

I was always lucky and the poor chap didn't really know what he was in for, as I always asked them if they could put the piece in place for me in the house, which was mostly on the second or third floor! However, I always gave them a bit more money and something to eat and drink. Well it worked. Job done.

Our dining room hosted a long Chippendale mahogany dining table with the usual silver candelabras, along with eight matching chairs, an antique sideboard, which was stunning with silver pots and platters, crystal decanters, and a serving trolley, along with incidental chairs and a bar area.

The drawing room was beautifully decorated, with old-fashioned sofas and armchairs in front of the open fire, along with the usual scattering of nest of tables and a long fire stool in front of the fire. Most colours of the curtains were gold and cream. Colours throughout the house were pretty neutral – creams and whites as a background canvas with splashes of colour for accessories and cushions.

Two of the bedrooms had four-posters, and then there was a twin-bedded room. The children's rooms were personalised for each with wallpaper full of animals and cars, and anything else they fancied at the time. Their rooms were a blur of colours, toys and books, teddies and cuddles on their beds, with duvets patterned with the 'rage' for their age!

It was here that my healing came through as a strong passion and my need to help others. Although throughout my life so far, I had helped animals first and then humans, now I was going on to another level. Being a mother is wonderful and a privilege, and our children teach us many lessons. The unconditional love is beautiful and very powerful.

They choose us parents for their lessons. It is natural for every mother to heal their children with words and hands on. Children naturally trust and accept. How many times when children fall over and hurt themselves do you say, "I will put my hand on the pain and take it away', or 'kiss it and make it better'? It works. And you know it.

So that is where healing starts. Children accept and know it anyway. We are all born with the gift of healing, it is just trusting and knowing it. It is good to use it all the time, otherwise you think you've lost it or didn't have it in the first place. Wrong! You can start again at any time, with the knowing that it is within you anyway, and put up that intention for whatever healing needs to be done. It comes through us, we are just vehicles for the energy that is channelled through us by source, higher powers, angels, God, Allah! Whatever your belief is. If you don't believe in higher powers, you must believe in energy. Well? Yes, that works!

Of course, conventional medicine plays its part when necessary, but alternatives and spiritual values are powerful additions, to work side by side with the medics. Watch your mind though, as it can play tricks! Always keep positive. Visualisation is a powerful tool. Visualise it and it will come about. Negativity will block its progress.

David was flying a lot and away for days at a time, and sometimes, as it goes with pilots' families, the wife often feels like a one-parent family, coping on her own in these long stretches.

We had decided to have an au pair to help me out, as there was a lot to do in the house and with the children. We had the best one ever, called Susan, who was totally competent in everything. She adored the children and they loved her in return.

As I had so much time on my own, I was lucky to have that time for my children. I definitely didn't want to go out to work, but I had the urge to do something for people that I would be able to do at home.

After a lot of thought, I took a beauty therapy course, which had quite tough exams for me, having flunked most of them at school! This time I was determined to get top marks. The anatomy and physiology ones were difficult, but with extra concentration, willpower, discipline and determination, I passed them all with top marks! Wow, that was a first!

After all the different body and facial treatments I could do, I then specialised in aromatherapy, which I loved. Throughout the course, I had already planned and set up one of the larger bedrooms and transformed it into a clinic. I brought in friends and friends of friends to practise on whilst I was still learning, so on completion of the course all these people stayed with me as clients, including referrals from many!

It was interesting, as quite a few of my clients would come in for a massage, facial or aromatherapy treatment and would very often tell me about health complaints they had, or pains persisting somewhere. As the most popular treatment would be aromatherapy, which actually treats mind, body and soul, I would address the part of the body that was in pain, using oils and touch. On many occasions the clients would come back saying that the pain, illness, or problems they had when they came the last time, had completely gone. My reputation grew and I was getting booked up in no time.

It was during this time that I met Jane at a neighbour's cocktail party. We became good friends very quickly and soon after meeting we regularly went to each other's houses for coffee, whilst the children all played together. She had two kids the same age as mine, so it was perfect.

Her husband, John, and David also got on very well together and, from time to time, we would have dinners at either our house or theirs. It was during one of these evenings, at the table, that Jane and I were talking about the work that I was doing. She was fascinated, and amazed at the results that I was having. "Oh wow, maybe you could help John?" she said.

Our husbands looked at each other with raised eyebrows; I had many of those as we were talking about healing and magic oils! Were we going to get a negative response here maybe? I then turned to John and asked him if I could help him.

He gingerly told me his story. For 10 years he had been suffering from an increasingly painful problem with his hips. This had been diagnosed as osteoarthritis, which had been aggravated (if not caused) by many years of playing football and squash. Since hip replacement operations last only 15-20 years, he had been advised that he should control the pain with painkillers thus delaying the operation as long as possible.

I then talked to him about what I did in the way of treatments, along with essential oils and healing through the hands. As I knew he was an industrial chemist by profession with a scientific background, I was treading very carefully and chose my words with care. I suggested to him that maybe he should see if a treatment would help him.

Some time passed after that get-together, and I got a call from him out of the blue to say that his wife had encouraged him to try a session with me, on a 'nothing ventured, nothing gained' premise. He was in a lot of pain, so last resort! "Can you book me in please?" Appointment swiftly made!

Even after only one treatment his condition improved dramatically. The pain in his hips, which somewhat restricted his mobility in walking and running, all but disappeared. A year later this remarkable improvement remained, after only four treatments in all.

His words: "I am no longer sceptical and whilst I have no idea, let alone explanation, as to how or why Zoë's treatment worked, I can testify to its efficiency. I would recommend to anyone with an ailment that either doesn't respond to conventional treatment, or for which the foreseeable treatment is fairly drastic, that they give Zoë an opportunity to surprise them with the incredible success of her treatment." Brilliant, another sceptic turned around!

"There is a purpose for everyone you meet."

- John Geiger

CHAPTER SEVEN

PARALLEL FRIENDS
Things that go bump in the night

So, what about that ghost? Well a few actually, throughout the years whilst at Moy Lodge. I always had the feeling of spirits around, and often got a glimpse of something like a flash of light, or a speck of colour, or different odours, or just a feeling. There was nothing nasty in the house, but there was something!

The children had the two bedrooms at the top of the house, next to each other; Vicky must have been around four years old and Charles five. Susan and I were sitting in the drawing room, relaxing after a hard day's work, when we heard noises coming from the top of the house. What on earth is that, I thought? The children had been fast asleep when we last checked! We sat and looked at each other for a few seconds then shot up to the top floor.

"Little monkeys," we said to each other as we were running up the stairs, "they are up playing with their toys!"

The noise was coming from Vicky's bedroom. We entered, with "back to bed please" on the tip of our tongues, when we saw the scene in front of us. The toys that had been put away at bedtime were now scattered all around the room. We quietly picked them all up and put them back in their place. Vicky was fast asleep in her bed, as was Charles when we peeped in. The ghosts must have had a field day!

One time when Susan and I were at the breakfast table with the children, Vicky casually said, as if it was a normal occurrence, "Who is that little girl that sits on my bed every night?" Susan and I looked at each other and thought here we go again!

Then the penny dropped! "It must be your guardian angel darling, sometimes they come to keep you company," I said. "Oh OK," she replied, "That's nice," and happily down she jumped off her chair and ran off with Charles to the playroom.

This is of course being the age when children can see their guardian angels and other angels. You know when your child asks if you can lay a place at the table for their friend and this friend has a name. This is real, and they shouldn't be discouraged. As long as you don't say 'there is no one there, it's your imagination, don't be silly' etc. etc. they will continue to see their angels and have their little conversations, and play with them.

The children's pure love and innocence will continue to see and just know they are there, until at maybe an age when they are stopped by adult intervention. Very often you can feel them around you without even seeing them, or just know. It is a knowing.

From time to time, I would hear a baby crying in the nursery. The old nursery was in the large bedroom next to ours on the second floor. This was the room that I used for my clinic. It had bars on the windows, which led us to the assumption that it was a nursery, then a playroom. I have to say I got anxious about the sound of a baby crying as it sounded distressed, but here again, it stopped each time I went into the room.

A story of life-changing moments

Myself and my children had had a lovely day out, visiting Chessington Zoo, and came back home tired and hungry. It was Susan's weekend off, so she had gone back to Ipswich to spend some time with her parents.

Having done the kids' supper, and spent time playing with bubbles in their bath, the three of us cosied up in Vicky's bed for stories. After giving in to, "Please, just one more Mummy," several times, it was more than enough. "OK, sleep time darlings," I said and tucked Vicky up and kissed her goodnight, then took Charles into his room and gave him a little more time before I kissed him goodnight and went downstairs.

An early night for me, I thought, so checked the children. Fast asleep. Did my usual rounds of locking the front and back doors, turning lights off around the house and went to bed.

I always left my bedroom door ajar so that I could hear the children as, from time to time, one of them would creep down and jump into bed with me. There was a night light on my landing in case they came down to go to the loo, which was on my floor. So, it was 'night night' to all, for a good night's sleep!

I was fast asleep when I was woken up by the sound of the pitter-patter of tiny feet on the stairs from the third floor. Thinking it was Vicky coming down to jump into bed with me, I lay still and looked towards my open door to say, "OK, in you pop."

Her little shadow from the landing night light appeared on the wall by my door, then disappeared. I heard her footsteps continue along the landing. I called out to her, no response; I thought she had gone to the loo, so I jumped out of bed to be with her.

No, she was not there, where did she go? I definitely didn't hear her go upstairs again, but would just check. I ran up the stairs and went straight into her room to find that she was fast asleep. Maybe it was Charles? No, he was fast asleep too.

For some time, I thought I was imagining things, or dreaming that this happened. The next time I heard the little feet coming down the stairs, I waited till I saw the shadow on the wall, then bolted out of my room to see who it was. Nothing there, nobody, then ran up to check the children. Yet again, they were fast asleep in their beds.

This happened many times, and each time I bolted out of bed to see who it was, the same thing always happened. I even tried talking to the 'presence', offering help of whatever it needed, but no, nothing. So, finally, it was an accepted reoccurrence, as it was with all of them.

"No, I haven't been smoking cigars in here," I replied to Susan, as she was complaining of the smell in the drawing room whilst we were hoovering and cleaning the room. "Anyway, it smells more like pipe tobacco. It reminds me of the odour that I had around me when I was with my grandfather, who smoked a pipe!" I replied.

"Well it is in here every morning when we come downstairs," she said. "How on earth are we going to get rid of it, and where is it coming from, the fire?" "Can't be, the log fire smells like it should, burning wood," I replied. A mystery!

It wasn't till quite some time later, when we had finished our day, put the children to bed, and went through to the kitchen to settle down and have our supper. We chatted for ages then decided it was time for bed. "Right," I said, "I am just going to the drawing room to check the windows are shut, then lock up."

As I walked into the drawing room, I shouted for Susan to come quickly. She arrived in seconds. Above the armchair, beside the fireplace, were little circles of smoke, and it was definitely the smell of pipe tobacco. It was moving upwards and spreading into little misty cloud shapes.

We were both speechless. What on earth is that? I thought. Could it be my grandfather trying to give me a message or what? Why is he here every night? Why does the odour linger every morning, if it's not real? Don't get it, yet!

When I first arrived at Moy Lodge, it was within a couple of weeks that I visited all the neighbours in our avenue, by knocking on their doors to introduce myself. This was a ritual I made with every move that we had, to collect friends! From that day on, I had around six families that continued to be good friends until we moved on.

I was particularly fond of an old lady who lived near to the entrance of our drive. I used to visit her regularly, either for a coffee or at cocktail time. She loved her G&Ts, so more often than not it was a 6pm visit! She lived on her own and welcomed the company.

It was over our G&Ts that she would talk about the history of the area, the stories of the neighbours, good or bad, and the local gossip from her cleaning lady and mobile hairdresser. She was fascinating to listen to and she knew everything that went on in the avenue, and more!

I got to know her very well, and we loved our times together. She had a great sense of humour and would laugh a lot. She was always so positive even when sometimes she would be in a lot of pain with her hips that gave her jip from time to time. She loved parties and would often have a few friends round for cocktails. Yup, she did remind me of Mummy!

One of the times, quite a while after we first met, we were having our usual G&Ts and putting the world to rights and catching up on gossip. "Did you know," she started, whilst sipping her drink, "that before Lady Cole's time, an admiral lived in your house?" "No, I didn't," I said, "I wonder if he is still in this area." "Highly unlikely, he died years ago," she replied.

Then she talked a little bit about him and his wife for a while, saying that he was a very stubborn man and his wife was lovely, but a bit bossy. Then laughing she said, "He used to irritate his wife like mad by smoking his cigars all over the house. Eventually she banned him from smoking in all rooms, bar the drawing room. So, believe it or not, that's where he spent most of his time, sitting in front of the fire, in peace with his pipe!"

"I believe it," I said. "Do you believe in ghosts?" "Yes," she said, and excitedly launched into a few of her experiences with them through the years. When she had finished her stories, I related the drawing room incident. "Well," she finally said, "probably it's a non-smoking zone where he is, so he just pops back now and then for a smoke!" then laughed her head off.

Sometimes when I went to bed at night, I thought 'please angels, let me have a full night's sleep without having to get up for something weird happening'. What had happened here for so many souls to be wandering around, and what should I do about it to help them?

One of the most annoying ones was the constant parties that were being held in the dining room below our bedroom. You could hear laughter and music and it went on and on. The first time it happened I was quite nervous to go downstairs. Oh, all right, scared out of my wits! It was so loud and obviously a lot of people down there! Go on, be brave, you know they won't hurt you, I told myself. What if they were all real people, they were not going to disappear with a flick of a switch!

It took me ages to get out of bed, thinking I have to go otherwise they won't stop. Or do I ring the police in case this is for real and I have an unsavoury gang of squatters down there, drunk and disorderly? No, the place is like Fort Knox, all windows double locked and doors the same.

OK then, off I go! I tiptoed downstairs very quietly and stood outside the dining room door and the chattering and music was still going on, but as soon as I opened the door there was no sound and no one there!

Occasionally when I was asleep, I would be awakened by horses and carriages driving past, under my bedroom window. I would jump out of bed to look out of the window, but never saw anything. I could still hear it for a while, including the cracking of a whip, but not a thing in view. Maybe it was King Henry VIII on his way to London!

David of course was usually never there when these things happened. But one day he was. I often used to tell him a little of what was going on, but it was, "Don't be ridiculous, it's all in your imagination. You're dreaming it."

He had come back from a trip and was very tired, so it wasn't late when we went to bed. In the middle of the night I was woken to the sound of music and parties under us in the dining room. Hopefully he wouldn't wake up, tired enough to sleep through it.

No such luck! "What's that bloody noise? I can't believe it, my first night back and this is what I get," he said. "I have told you before," I said, "this goes on a lot of the time when you are away, they have parties and are chatting and singing to music in the dining room. It's our ghosts, but they won't harm us. They're having fun. I am used to it."

Furious, he said, "You stupid woman, you have left the television on. Go and turn it off." "No, I haven't," I replied. "You don't believe me, so go and turn it off yourself." With that he flew down in temper, and when he heard the music coming from the dining room and not the drawing room, he obviously reached for the door of the dining room and opened it. Yup, silence. "So," I said, as he jumped back into bed. "Go to sleep," he replied. Stuck for words? I could practically see his white face glowing in the dark.

I had a very good friend who offered to come and babysit the house for us when we were on holiday. When we returned, she told me about some of the 'things that went bump in the night', so I had confirmation that they really did happen, and it wasn't my imagination. Needless to say, she only did it once! She vowed she would never stay at Moy Lodge again on her own!

Anyway, I loved Moy Lodge and found it very hard to leave it when we left for Bahrain. David had done all the interviews with Gulf Air and soon we would be off *en famille*. Exciting – a new venture in a new country.

Moy Lodge was being let out to a large company; thank goodness, we were able to keep it, to come home to after our contract. Before we left, I got anxious about our floating residents, never mind the human residents about to come in, so I researched for an exorcist for this kind of work to free the spirits so they could return in peace.

Eventually I found one in the nick of time. She was a lovely old lady and obviously very experienced in what she did. She walked through the house and led me up to Vicky's bedroom on the third floor. Here we sat cross-legged on the floor in front of each other, and she did some prayers and chants. We sat in silence for a while, and then we heard all sorts of noises whooshing past us and upwards. Nothing scary, sort of voices of thanks and a feeling of relief to us, knowing that my friends would be OK now and at peace.

Packing up Moy Lodge was an absolute nightmare, and of course I couldn't get rid of the sentimental stuff, such as baby clothes, certain cuddles, heirlooms etc. etc. Crates and crates were put into storage at vast expense. Well, I thought, it will only be for three years and then I will see it all again! However, I had a gut feeling it would be much longer than that!

We paid our last visit to Scotland to say our goodbyes and it was all very emotional. Daddy kept stressing that we were going into the middle of a war zone, and it wasn't safe. Mummy was crying and Zandra was devastated! It can be a difficult thing with the separation of identical twins; it was like leaving part of me behind! However, we knew that we could tune into each other so we would always know when one or the other needed help. We stressed that we would be back regularly for holidays, and speak on the phone every week. There were no emails in those days, so those were the only choices we had.

"Your angels are ALWAYS with you, every minute of every day. You are never alone. You are loved and watched-over."

- Doreen Virtue

CHAPTER EIGHT

THE ISLANDS OF BAHRAIN
Life in the glorious desert

David had already flown to Bahrain to suss out the accommodation for us, so we were already allocated a house within a Gulf Air compound. The children were really excited about this new adventure and, I have to say, so was I. Here we go!

When we disembarked the plane at Bahrain, the heat hit us with its intensity. Fab, I thought, I love the heat, it can never be too hot for me! I had that lovely feeling that one often gets in a special place, of 'coming home'! A past life maybe? Little did I know that this three-year contract would turn into 10 years of some of the happiest times in my life!

Driving along to our new home wasn't too far and, in those days, there were very few houses along the way. Looking around, there was sand, sand, and more sand, with palm trees dotted around, along with camels meandering in all directions.

I thought we were in the middle of the desert, and yes indeed we were. At last we arrived at our destination. A huddle of not very pretty houses, more like shacks, I thought, of around 10 bunched together, with no sign of life! "You won't like this, not what we are used to," said David. Ain't that the truth, I thought, and for once I was speechless.

There we were in the middle of the desert, far away from the town, and all in this little huddle of run-down houses. 'Custer's Last Stand', which I found out later was the name our neighbours had nicknamed it!

In we went with our suitcases, and indeed it was dated, with the bare necessities. Not quite my style: basic kitchen with a back door leading to a small tatty sandy back yard, overlooking the desert with many small and large sand mounds, some of which I assumed could be burial mounds. There was a separate dining room leading out from the kitchen, a very sparse living room with out-of-date Ikea hand-downs, a narrow staircase going up to three dreary bedrooms with wonky wardrobes and drawers and certainly not much storage space anywhere.

The children were delighted and excited, they thought they had arrived at one huge sand pit! Here we had residents galore, of the creepy crawly kind, in and out of the house. Certainly not like our last ones in Moy Lodge but ones that we could definitely see.

It took a while to get used to the cockroaches that we found scuttling around the house, especially in the kitchen. The gecko lizards were gorgeous and we loved them. They ran up and down the walls and across the ceilings and were good to have around as they ate the nasty little insects, like mosquitos, that flew their way.

The desert rats weren't very nice, but it was the camel spiders that freaked me out. I don't like spiders! This was on our doorstep. In fact, under our doorstep there was a nest of camel spiders, which were unbelievable creatures, and I hated them. I had the 'heebie-jeebies' trying to jump over the doorstep going in and out of the house!

They were big and crab like, sort of translucent in colour, and could run up to 30mph. If you ran away from them, they would run after you. No, they don't want you, they want your shade! When a person runs, the camel spider will chase the shadow. If a person stands still, the camel spider will too, enjoying the cool. This is how they got their name, from standing under camels for the cool of the shade. Their bite is not venomous, however, but they inject an anaesthetic into you so you won't feel anything, and then they eat the flesh. Yuck!

I heard a story about one of the stewardesses who was lying by the pool, sunbathing, and fell asleep. When she woke up, she had a chunk of flesh from her leg bitten away. The camel spider had crept up, given her the anaesthetic then munched his breakfast and ran away at top speed! Vicky loved insects and many a time I had to stop her reaching out to pick up a scorpion. The desert snakes were OK and didn't really bother us as they slithered all over the place and occasionally in the house.

David had already bought me a blue open jeep, like the ones you saw in the *M*A*S*H* television series, and that was where we had the most fun, driving over the desert. Charles was around six and Vicky five, so everything was an adventure, even going to school.

I used to drive them in the jeep, with an extra tour around the mounds and over the smaller ones. We would have a lizard-counting game. The desert lizards were huge and they came out of the sand and mounds in the early morning, then when they saw us, they would run away at the speed of lightning.

If we were running late to school, we would drive around the mounds. Going to school was fun; quite near to the school there was an Arabic bread oven walled in brick with a little man throwing the bread at the sides of the oven. We always stopped there and had hot plain naans, or those with melted cheese in them. The children loved them and munched away along the bumpy ride ahead. Yummy start to school.

Our neighbours were delightful, and as all expats do when we are thrown together, we quickly get to know each other and are there for support at all times. I just couldn't believe the entertaining that went on. Every night there were sundowners and drinks in each house, taking turns, dinner parties, cocktail parties, and pool parties, with children of all ages joining in.

I had decided that I was going to turn the dining room into a clinic! There I could treat all the housewives with relaxing and healing treatments. A lot of them got bored when their husbands were flying on long trips, so this would be a good idea. I don't think David was that keen to begin with, but he eventually went along with it.

I soon became very busy whilst the children were at school. With word of mouth, clients were coming in regularly. There was one lady I was giving an aromatherapy treatment to who had been suffering from a pain in her back that she had had for a long time and had tried medicines and various treatments to no avail. I said I would rebalance her then concentrate on her back, which I did.

As I had my hands on her, she said, "You are a healer. I know you are; I can feel the pain going away." "It's not me," I said, "I am just the vehicle for the healing energy that is going to you from source." "How do you know it is going to work?" she said. "I just know. It's a 'knowing' feeling," I replied. From that day she never had any more pain. From this happening, many of the expats heard about what I was doing, and little by little I was inundated over the 10 years that I was there.

One night over sundowners at one of my neighbours, hosted by a captain and his wife Sandy, who was headmistress of St Christopher's, the children's school, Sandy introduced me to her housekeeper, Ashok, who had been working for them for around a year. Everyone had a housekeeper in those days. He was an absolutely charming Indian aged 18 years.

Sandy said that he had some free hours and asked if I would like to take him on. Absolutely, no housework, no cooking, just the occasional baby-sitting. What more could I want! He was a delight to have in the house, and we all treated him like a member of the family. He was like a son to me, young and naive. He stayed with us then and throughout our different moves around Bahrain until our final departure.

The children and I were always having little adventures whilst David was away, touring around the desert in the jeep, over bumps and hills, with great excitement and glee, the children squealing "faster, faster" as the bumps bumped them up into the air and down on their seats again.

This particular time, we had gone for a walk in the desert, passing little villages and from time to time chatting to the locals. The Bahrainis loved children and we had admiration voiced to my little ones, with pats on their heads and huge smiles of warmth.

When we were walking along on our own, we spotted a forlorn donkey standing on his own. Once we got near to him, our hearts sank. He was skeleton thin with welts, cuts and scars all over his body. Totally undernourished and very sad.

"Right," I said to Charles and Vicky, "we have to take him home and feed him up and heal him!" We got him home, leading him by a tatty threadbare rope that was around his neck. He could hardly walk, but slowly by slowly we arrived at our house and put him in the back yard.

"Oh no madam," Ashok said, "Sir will not like." Well sir didn't like, when he got back from his trip, but allowed us to have him until he was taken by the BSPCA. Well that was difficult in itself; I phoned around to see who was responsible for rescuing animals and couldn't find anyone.

Meantime we fed him up, bathed his sores, talked and cuddled him, and healed him back to health. He became very friendly and certainly one of the family. He even walked through the open door of the kitchen to steal anything that looked like a carrot on the kitchen tops.

The strangest thing with him was that he couldn't make the 'haw' sound, so when he called to us, we heard this bellowing 'hee', with a breath sound for the 'haw'. So, of course, we called him Hee! I would spend several hours at a time talking to him and tuning into him to find out what had happened, and putting my hands on him with the intent of ridding him of his trauma. Little by little he recovered totally and exchanged his gratitude with love and trust. Eventually we found him a good home.

After living three years there, I had certainly had enough of this make-do home, especially having seen how the other half lived in their very acceptable Gulf Air accommodation. The last straw was when our creepy-crawly residents continued to enjoy our home and garden, no matter what we did to try and get rid of them. In despair now and really fed up with trying to keep the children away from the nasty ones, I asked David to put a

A story of life-changing moments

request into the Head of Housing for us to move. Eventually the request came back and had been refused. I went mad. Right, that's it!

I went around the house with gloves on and collected cockroaches, and as many of the inhabitants that I could of the creepy kind, into a large jar. Off at top speed in my jeep to Housing. Nothing to lose, I thought, just go for it! When I arrived there, jar in hand, I asked the secretary if I could see the manager. "No, you need an appointment." I saw someone come out of his room and leave the office. "Is that the manager's office?" I said, looking at the now closed door.

"Yes," she said, and with that I barged into his office, unscrewed the jar, and tipped the contents of the creepies on to his desk, with words of distress coming out all at once, saying, "These are not on our inventory and I want to move, it is not healthy for our children, and if we don't move I am leaving and going back to the UK with the children, and then you will have an unhappy captain."

Then I sat down on the chair in front of his desk and burst into tears, with a few hysterics thrown in. When I got home and told David what I had done, he was horrified, and said, "You can't do that, we will all be chucked out of here now." "We'll be fine," I said, "deed is done." Having won an Oscar for my performance in the housing office, we had the notice of our move within a couple of weeks. Whew!

"Begin with an open mind, end with an inspired heart."

- Sheri Fink

CHAPTER NINE

SINKING IN QUICKSAND
Healing gifts and intervention

Our next home was a dream, again a bit shabby but it was in old colonial style within a gated and guarded compound, including a large swimming pool and tennis court. It had outside maids' quarters that were run down and derelict so, as Ashok came with us, he stayed in accommodation nearby. The rooms were large and we had plenty of space with four bedrooms.

The lounge-diner was plenty big enough to swing many cats, of which we had two. One, a moggie called Candy, we inherited from our house where the last owners left it on the doorstep. Another, a Siamese called Catastrophe that we were given by a friend who was leaving Bahrain, was a serious catastrophe, getting into all sorts of trouble. She used to throw herself at the curtains in the lounge, shoot up them then fling herself down.

She was always having accidents, one of them being falling from a tree and breaking a leg. It was out of surgery hours when this happened. Now what do I do, I thought. An idea came to me in moments, so I wrapped her up in a towel and took her to the A&E department at the local hospital. I walked in with her cuddled up like a baby, and sat down in the waiting room trying to look invisible!

Everyone thought it was my baby! When I was taken through to the medics, to their horror and disbelief, they saw it was a cat! I pleaded with them to do something, and do you know, they did, and put her leg in a cast! Well I can't think of anywhere else in the world that would happen!

David was very fond of birds and he acquired an African grey baby parrot, Priscilla, which we reared. This was David's soul mate, and I am quite sure she came before me in the pecking order! They soon became inseparable and he spent hours with her.

She would fly around the house as she pleased, chewing on wires, landing on David's shoulder at every opportunity, and very often remaining there at meal times whilst he hand-fed her bits of food from his dinner plate. At night times she went back to her cage. Very quickly she started talking and mimicked everything she could, until later through the years she could practically have a conversation with you.

It was at this time that Charles went off to Cranleigh boarding school in the UK. Most of the expatriate children had to do this to get the best from their education, as there weren't the facilities in Bahrain at that time. Taking him there was heartbreaking and all along I was trying to make it an exciting adventure for him. I will never forget when I settled him in for the first time and leaving him there with his favourite cuddly under his arm. He was only eight but the headmaster had said it was the best age for the boys to be able to settle in well.

Vicky was later and she went to St Catherine's at age ten. I was back in England at that time staying in Addlestone prior to settling her in when Julie, a neighbour friend of mine, took her to the park whilst I was doing last-minute things, like sewing name tags on her clothes, when I got a call from her saying that they were in A&E as Vicky had fallen badly and broken her leg.

Horrors! I flew out of the door to get there as quickly as possible. My poor baby was in agony and I sat beside her hospital bed while she was crying her eyes out. It was a bad break and a cast was put on. After a week, when she was due to start school, I was in a dilemma as to whether to let her go or not. However, the doctor said she was fine and of course I didn't think it wise for her not to be there at the beginning so she didn't miss out on making friends quickly.

So off we went and I settled her into her dormitory. The matron and all the girls were marvellous, and she had attention and help with everything as she struggled a bit with doing things on her crutches. Yes, that was the best decision. Throughout the term times, I would always say, "I will be with you every time you go to bed at night and you will feel me tickle your feet!" They always said they did. I wonder if they said that just to comfort me.

Luckily, they both loved their schools, and of course had the best of both worlds to be able to travel extensively with us and have a home in an exciting place, which led to envy from their school friends, several of which visited on holidays. I went back for exeats when I could and half terms. We had acquired a little pied-à-terre in Addlestone on the canal, which served as our UK base during our overseas postings. Perfect.

So, we were now very settled in our new compound, with lovely neighbours, some of whom were from our old compound, and I had more clients coming in for help. This was becoming a bit intrusive in our home life, so I had an idea! David had just gone off on a two-week trip when I said to Ashok, "Can you get hold of some workmen for me, to convert the staff quarters into a clinic?" He said, "Yes madam, but what will sir say?" "He'll be fine," I replied, "we have two weeks starting from now."

Well, it was a bit of a nightmare; it was a fairly small room but big enough to get a treatment bed in, a chair, a small table, and a trolley for my aromatherapy oils. From off this room there was a stand-up and do-it-yourself, hole in the ground loo, which stank of sewage! That would definitely have to be blocked. Yuck, could be difficult!

The workmen duly came in and worked like trojans. Walls painted white, adorned with certificates of different therapies, white doors, and pale green carpet laid on the floor. Loo cemented over and a floor laid, providing a space for storage, door shut.

Quickly the place was ready for work, with clients booked in before David came home. "What!" he said, "you can't do that, it's not legal, I will be sacked and you'll have your hands cut off…" adding a few descriptive adjectives in between. "We'll be fine," as you know, was my usual answer.

From then, I started filling up appointments with those that had aches and pains and other problems. The amount of secrets that were locked in behind the doors made me not only a counsellor but an agony aunt as well.

One day I was looking out of the window, watching out for my new client to take him next door for his treatment. He had phoned in for a treatment and just given his first name. He had a pain from an old injury to his arm, and he had tried everything and seen many doctors but it just wouldn't go away.

He had had it for a very long time, and it was getting him down. I saw the guards open the gates and a posh chauffeur-driven car came in. Who on earth is that? I thought. Oh, it's my client, he's stopping at my front door. I went out to meet him then ushered him into my forbidden clinic! He was obviously of great importance, so I handled my words with care.

As I was doing the hands-on healing on his arm, I concentrated on the injury and felt the heat coming through. It was very hot for him, and like many, he said that it was like a hot water bottle resting on his arm. After the treatment he said that the pain had reduced by half. I advised him to come back for a couple more sessions to make sure that there was no pain left.

After a couple more treatments the pain had totally disappeared. He was astonished and said, "This is a miracle." He loved having the treatments and each time he also felt other ailments going plus having an amazing deep sleep every night. He became one of my regulars, in addition to sending some of his friends to me. He also said to me that I was doing a great job for people and I would be safe in my business whilst I was on the island.

Yes, miracles happen, and I began to see more and more.

It was a magical day when he came in again. We did the treatment, and as usual had our lovely chats, when at the end he said to me, "I have a present for you, to thank you for the miracle you helped to make happen for me. I am so grateful and I want to give you something special. I am giving you two Arab horses to ride. One for you, and I know you want to teach your daughter to ride, so one is for her. You can go to my stables any time and the grooms will have your horses tacked up for you ready to ride. The horses' names are Alhardy and O'Brian. They are for your use for as long as you are here in Bahrain."

I was near to tears, and thanked him over and over. I was numb and speechless apart from continuous thank yous. I was so excited, I couldn't wait to tell Vicky, who would definitely be over the moon. It was like a dream come true for me and Vicky. We both adored horses. Brilliant.

Having had the horses for a while and managing to get out with them every day, we were ready for another adventure. A few more lessons for Vicky, which I gave to her on Alhardy with me by her side on O'Brian, and then we were off, literarily into the sunset.

Yes, you're right! Sunrise and sunset were our favourite times for our rides. There's nothing like riding across the desert with the sun coming up or going down. Magical! One of our favourite rides was to the beach. There was one day we shall never forget! Vicky and I collected our horses and set off towards the beach. It was so special there, with the feeling of peace and belonging to "All That Is".That's what you have when standing at the edge of the sea. This is the place where thousands of angels congregate, and you can actually feel it if you empty your thoughts and just feel how you feel!

Watching the waves and hearing the sound of them, being carried away on the waves of bliss, encircled by nature at its magnificent best.

It was a fabulous morning and we chatted away as we were trotting along. From time to time we would canter or gallop, depending on the conditions of the ground. When galloping in the desert we had to take care of the stony areas that could potentially trip us up.

"Shall we go into the sea today?" I said to Vicky. "Yes please," was the reply, so that we did. It was a great feeling of the splashing of water around the horses' legs and on to us as we walked in.

A story of life-changing moments

The horses were loving it. What a magical feeling of freedom as we were swishing along, side by side.

Chatting and laughing, we were having a great time, and promised to each other that we would do this more often. All of a sudden, our horses got jittery and were finding it difficult to walk on. Walk on, they couldn't even walk. We were sinking, and sinking fast. Oh no, we were in a quicksand!

We were right in that feeling of a dreaded nightmare, almost frozen, to 'this can't be happening to us'. Now what? Vicky was screaming and absolutely terrified, the horses were shaking in panic, and I was numb and asking for help from God, my angels, and everyone.

Stop thinking and act, act now! I told myself. The water was up to near enough the horses' shoulders, and I shouted to Vicky, "Hang on and stay on. We will be OK!" I swiftly jumped off my horse and miraculously landed on a firmer area of the sea bed. Even so, I felt that I might be sinking down at any time. I grabbed both the horses' reins and pulled them like mad to get them on the firm sand. The horses were scrambling in fear, you could see it in their eyes, and trying desperately to free their legs from the grabbing sands. Little by little there seemed to be less water up their bodies, and slowly I managed to pull them on to sound ground and out of danger. I must have had an extra hand in this! Divine intervention, for sure!

Vicky leapt off her horse and ran into my arms. The four of us were trembling and cuddling into each other as tight as we could, in the silence following the terror of what had just happened. The only thing I could think of now was to get that trauma out of our bodies as quickly as possible.

"OK darling, back on your horse. I will race you back to the stables," I said. We mounted as fast as we could and shot off like bullets towards the yard, and got there at the speed of lightning. Probably the fastest gallop that we had ever had, all four of us!

Of course, animals can rid traumas from their bodies when confronted with danger. They shake profusely with the fear that they are feeling, and then bolt off as fast as they can into the distance. This helps to rid the traumas out of their bodies. We should all take a leaf out of their book. So that is exactly what I was trying to do!

When we got back to the stables, we told the grooms what had happened. They were shocked and then reluctantly proceeded to tell us that two people had lost their lives in that part of the sea a year or so earlier.

As if we didn't have enough mess in the house already with Priscilla, David then brought home a cockatoo that he saw in the window of a pet shop whilst out shopping and felt sorry for it, so bought it on the spot!

In addition, at almost the same time, we acquired a huge Malaccan called Baby from a guy who owned an Irish pub in the centre of Bahrain and was about to leave the island. He was on a search to find a good home for her, and to his relief found one whilst talking to David over a pint at his bar!

One of our neighbours was also leaving, and gave us her two budgerigars as a present, and by this time it was full house! Are we starting a zoo here or what, I thought. Memories of my childhood coming up! The cats and the birds ignored each other most of the time luckily, although Catastrophe felt superior to them all, and at times hissed and clawed herself up the curtains at great speed, as if on a mission, with her nose in the air!

Baby was gorgeous, and although Malaccans' beaks can be pretty lethal, she was very gentle and would cuddle into our chests and go to sleep. All the birds had the freedom to fly around the house, perching on shoulders, lampshades, sofas and beds!

Priscilla by this time was mimicking beautifully, and her vocabulary was growing. She was word perfect with the sounds of the telephone ringing, David's voice of "Ooo yahs," (from David, when he hurt himself or jolted with back pain). "Who's a clever girl then? Vicky broke her leg, poor Vicky. Who's that? No more drink Daddy, night night Mummy," and then she would burp and say, "Whoops sorry." In addition, we did have a few of my husband's colourful adjectives thrown in! Just as well my clinic was outside of the house and away from our feathered friends!

There was one time, when David and I decided to go out for dinner. Charles was at boarding school and Vicky was staying with a school friend. We went into town for dinner and came home fairly late. When we walked into the house, we felt that something was not quite right as things had been moved around. Many objects were not in the right place and drawers of cupboards were open. We checked the back door to find it had been forced open, then of course we realised that there had been an attempted burglary.

On careful inspection throughout, it looked as if the intruders had been in for a very short time, and obviously had left in a hurry. Nothing was missing and there was no damage, so we felt there was no need to call the police. "How strange is that?" David said. "They have taken nothing. What stopped them?" Then it dawned on me. I replied, "I bet you anything they heard your voice saying 'who's that, who's that?'" Guard Bird Priscilla? Saved by the squawk!

> *"You don't have to be an angel, just be someone who can give."*
>
> *- Patti LaBelle*

88 HANDS ON FOREVER   *A story of life-changing moments*

CHAPTER TEN

AN ARAB BOY'S DREAM
The last miracle in Bahrain

A couple of years later we moved into town to a large house with amazing character, masses of space, marble floors and a spiral staircase going up to four good-sized bedrooms. There was a separate staff room at the side of the house, with its own entrance for patients; as per normal for me, I had converted it into a clinic, and our feathered friends luckily were cut off from my working areas.

One day I received a phone call from a local lady, and she spoke so fast with desperation in her voice that I could hardly understand what she was saying. "Slow down, slow down," I said.

Her story was, "I got your name from a friend of mine who has urged me to come and see you. It's for my son actually. He is eight years old and has been in Great Ormond Street Hospital in the UK undergoing treatments for a long time now. They say that there is no more they can do for him. Please help me, I have heard about the success you have had with many people. Please can you see him?"

She then told me that he was dwarfed as his bones were not growing and he was like a sparrow of half his age. He had chronic asthma and eczema, and was very introverted. "Of course," I said, and made an appointment for them.

Poor little chap. When I saw him, my heart went out to him, and his mother was absolutely distraught beyond words. He was small and thin, covered in eczema with red patches all over him. I put him on the treatment bed and started a healing session; his skin was raw in many places and it was apparent that his confidence was minimal. Well, the first place I have to start with is his head, I thought, to bring him some positivity and hope, and that would mirror his mother also.

He came to me for treatments each week. The first couple of times, he was reluctant to leave the skirts of his mother, hanging on to them in silence of distrust and fear. Then little by little, the little miracles happened.

It was not very long before he gained his trust in me and would fly through the door flinging himself into my arms, with a smile on his face and excited to continue our fun times. Yes, it was fun for him, and this is what I did.

By this time, he was happy to be in the room with me on our own whilst his mother would sit next door. I had said to her to keep positive at all times for him and for herself. Just know that he will get better, little by little.

First of all, he would sit on a chair opposite me, and we would chat about all the fun things he liked to do. Gradually we brought out his dream, of ice skating. He wanted to be a famous ice skater, and while he talked about it his eyes lit up.

We then went into story land and I said that we would have a different chapter every week. The story began at the beginning, telling him of how he put his skates on for the first time, and the feeling of excitement when he stood on the ice for the first time.

A story of life-changing moments

Then the story progressed, as did his dream. Each week there was a new chapter of improvement, followed by improvement in his body.

The second half of the session, he went eagerly on to the treatment bed to dream about this chapter and beyond whilst I had my hands on his body, healing him. He would go to sleep, and then at the end wake up refreshed, happy and positive.

Each week the story got a little further, and the symptoms on his body got a little less. He was so excited to hear the next episode as we knew that we were going towards the gold medal for his ice skating.

By this stage of his story we were winning competitions with him actually dancing on ice. His mother was thrilled with his progress, and she too became more positive. After a few weeks, when he had won his gold medal, he saw me regularly for maintenance, and top-ups of fun.

One day, his mother rang me and said, "I have just been to the International Hospital for my son to have his regular check-up. The two specialists from London who had been treating him there were back to check his progress. They couldn't believe the improvement in his body and also that he was so positive and happy. They asked me what I was doing to make this vast difference, so I told them about you. They have asked me to ask you if they could come and watch you in session, as they are fascinated in what you do!" Ah, what do I say to her? not really, but OK? They will probably think I am doing 'witchity poo stuff' as my husband used to say to me in jest! "Yes, of course," I said to her, "no problem."

The day came, and I was dreading it. These two eminent specialists coming to watch me tell stories to a little boy, put him on the bed to lay my hands on him, and close my eyes for the other half hour whilst moving my hands up and down his body! Right, I thought, I won't be intimidated as I know it works, and that's all there is to it. Help, angels! I'll be fine!

In they came with mother and child. Pleasant introductions, and actually they were charming. Whew! I took the guys aside and said, "The only thing I stipulate is that you say nothing to me or the boy whilst we are in session, and then we can speak afterwards." "Absolutely," they replied. The mother went to the next room and the boy and the professionals came into session with me. Nothing changed with our session, a fun half hour then healing. The boy and I engrossed in our story, didn't even feel we had company. For the healing, I just focused, closed my eyes, put the intention up to my angels and left it to them to channel the healing through the vehicle which was me. Great, all done. A happy little boy who then ran to the other room to wait with his mother.

To my surprise, one of the specialists said to me, "I don't totally understand how you do this or what you do, but the results are amazing. The boy is all yours, and we are handing him over to you. Thank you for all your good work." They shook hands with me and left in silence. From then on, my little Arab boy started growing, with all his symptoms diminishing.

That dreaded day had arrived when the news broke out that a possible war was imminent. Precautionary measures had already been made, and all expatriate families had been issued with gas masks. In addition, the windows throughout each property had been sealed around the edges with tape to prevent any possible poisonous gas seeping through.

The children, around 12 and 13 now, had two school friends, Gemma and Damian, staying for two weeks during this summer holiday. They were having a ball, swimming, boating, playing tennis, watching movies, and thoroughly enjoying their time together. David was away on a trip, and we were packing activities in, to the maximum, before their holidays ended.

The British embassy was going to let us know should we have to evacuate quickly, so at this point I thought I had better get the children's friends on a plane to London as soon as possible.

They beat me to it! Both mothers rang me within minutes of each other, to say, "What is happening over there? It sounds bad from the news we are getting in the UK." It was pretty much the same words from both of them. We decided that I would get the tickets as soon as possible, and put them on the plane to go home. I reassured them that my kids and I would follow on as soon as we could. Immediately I got off the phone, I rang Gulf Air and got the first two seats booked with no trouble. The next day they left.

Soon after I received a phone call to say get out now, as there is a rumour flying around that the gas is going to be dropped over Bahrain this afternoon. Oh no, evacuation had started. Ashok and I were in shock, and I felt that horrible sick panicky feeling rising up from my stomach.

Where is David? I wondered. I couldn't get hold of him, he was on a trip but I couldn't remember exactly where, and had no time to check. I would try and get hold of him later. Then I ran in circles for a while, not knowing what to do first!

I rang Gulf Air to get a flight out for the three of us, but all the planes were fully booked. It was impossible. What happened to 'women and children first'? Then I rang a friend of mine who worked in the British Airways office to ask for her help. She said that there were no availabilities for London, it was fully booked, and the only three seats left to anywhere now was Abu Dhabi. "OK, I'll take those," I said. No problem, I thought, I can get an onward flight to London from there. She said, "Come and get the tickets now, as you only have a couple of hours before you have to be at the airport."

Trying not to show a wobble in my voice, so as not to worry the children, I said to them, "Get packed, Ashok will help you and I will be back soon. Then we will fly to Abu Dhabi for a night, stop there, then on to London tomorrow morning."

I asked Ashok to help the kids pack, and have three small pieces of hand luggage ready for my return. "Only put in the children's favourite things with clothes for one night, mine the same with all my jewellery. Nothing else, we must travel light." Ashok was getting really anxious as he was going to be left on his own, and his fear of maybe not seeing us again was welling up.

I drove like a lunatic to the BA office, but the streets in town were jammed in many directions and parking everywhere was impossible. I felt the minutes ticking by, thinking this is a nightmare! Whew, got there, parked somewhere I thought was illegal. Too bad, nobody would care in this situation, ran into the office and got our tickets.

Then of course I had to get money from the bank. Oh, this was definitely impossible. The crowds were thickening and everyone was panicking. Got to the bank but the queues were enormous with people filing outside the building. Fights had started in the streets, people screaming and shouting, as everyone tried to barge their way into the bank to get their money out.

No time now, I had to go, so I ran to my car and drove at top speed back to the house. I was late getting back and Ashok was waiting on the doorstep with Charles and Vicky, plus three small cabin bags. We hugged Ashok for as long as we could, I told him not to worry, that we would be fine and would see him

A story of life-changing moments

soon. That he didn't believe, from the sad look he had on his face, as we then had to leave him in floods of tears on the doorstep. Now we were all in tears.

Whew, we just caught the plane in the nick of time. It was chock-a-block of course, and off we went. The atmosphere of fear was thick in the plane, fear of scuds maybe flying past us, or being shot down, and everything else the imagination would conjure up. I kept thinking, will we ever get through this, what's going to happen next? Will we ever see our families again? Oh, I haven't got any money, where will we go when we get there? Where shall we stay? Ah, the crew hotel, and surely, I will find someone on the crew I know, that will help us.

Trying to chat normally to the children and make it a fun adventure was difficult with the negative energies building up in the cabin during our flight. Silences part of the time around us, noises of tears and fears, with everyone wearing grim expressions and hanging on to their armrests, with the possible expectations of doom. The stewardesses were well up to scratch, serving refreshments with smiles, and keeping busy with the full load. Eventually we got there, it seemed a very long flight. The first thing we heard from people chatting on the ground was that the gas could be dropped here first, before Bahrain! Right, we needed a flight back to London as soon as possible.

The children were tired when we got to the hotel where the crew were staying. I asked the receptionist if I could see the crew list, as I was the wife of one of the Gulf Air captains, to see if I knew anyone there or coming in. "Of course," she said and showed me the list. Lo and behold, I saw my husband's name on it, arriving in around an hour. Brilliant! Having pointed this out to the receptionist, I asked her for the key to his room so I could wait there with the children until he arrived.

Saved by the captain! David duly arrived. He was very surprised that we had flown there to get back to London and more surprised that we were waiting for him in his room! He immediately organised a flight for us for the following morning.

The children were feeling happy and safe, knowing that Daddy would fix everything and all would be OK. Off we went the next day, the children very excited as we were going home to safety and they would be seeing their school friends.

I stayed in the UK for quite some time then, and David remained in Bahrain with his gas mask and Priscilla his parrot at his side! Actually, he also had another female bird by his side at that time, of the human kind, I found out later!

As it often happens in a war situation when guys are left on their own, they seem to take comfort and solace elsewhere (not with a parrot!), without their wives and children beside them. Well, life is like that and you just have to get through it and out the other side. My angels have always guided and helped me.

David is a great father and provider, with a great sense of humour, highly intelligent, funny, fun, and always does his best for the family and more. I will always love him and we were soul mates. The history between us is huge and that can't ever be taken away. But for me, at that point in time, my heart was sinking. Nevertheless, we stayed together. The gas never came down and Bahrain was safe again. It was time to move on. This was the end of our 10 year stay in Bahrain.

"Out of difficulties grow miracles."

- Jean de la Bruyere

SINGAPORE
Moving East and opening new doors

David had now joined Singapore Airways, so our new adventure was moving to Singapore. It was an exciting place, and the children – well, teenagers by now – loved it. We were ready for a change and welcomed this new culture. We had a fabulous house on the east coast, walking distance to the sea. When we arrived there first, it was like walking out of the plane into a sauna, around 35° with around 95% humidity.

Then what struck us most was the amazing greenery and colour of various tropical plants, beautifully landscaped at the borders of the roads, and the palm trees in abundance scattered all around. The smell of the sea and the chirping of the local birds was a song to one's ears. I thought Priscilla will have a field day when she comes here!

Our house was large with four spacious bedrooms and an open-plan drawing room that led to the dining area. French windows opened onto the back patio and garden beyond, with a few local inhabitants including the occasional python or cobra.

The kitchen wasn't huge, but that didn't matter to me one bit as I wasn't in it a lot! We had a gorgeous Indian housekeeper called Sara who did most of the cooking for us. Her speciality was of course curry, which was amazing. She used to spend a day cooking the different dishes then follow me around the house after each finished item, with a few tasters on a plate, saying, "taste, madam." All were delicious. Then she would repeat the same tour with the next culinary delight.

Once we were all settled in our brand new and refurnished house, with all its oriental charms such as standing lanterns from Korea that were used as side lights, a divine lacquered bar, posh sofa sets, an amazing long dining table with eight matching ornate chairs, beds with suspended mosquito nets that were just for show and lots of beautiful eastern blue and white china – it looked as if we had been in Singapore for a lifetime.

The house gleamed from the care of Sara, from the pristine clean and polished wood to an immaculate kitchen floor that you could practically eat off. She also took care of organising our wardrobes and the washing and ironing galore, in addition to making the beds with fresh linen. How will I ever get used to not having servants when we eventually return to the UK, I wondered. Horrors! But we treated her as family, as we did with Ashok who unfortunately had to stay behind in Bahrain. He was like a son to me over the 10 years and even though we looked into all possibilities to bring him with us, it was to no avail.

So now it was time for Priscilla to come over from Bahrain; she had in the meantime been looked after by a friend until it was the right timing for her to join us in Singapore. Now I wondered how long it would be before the showroom of a house turned into an open cage for a messy destructive bird! The rest of our birds in Bahrain were given away before we left. Just as well maybe!

A story of life-changing moments

However, David was adamant in bringing the 'love of his life' with him, Priscilla!

Her flight to Singapore was exciting for her, as my husband flew her over in his plane, and she sat on his shoulder in the cockpit, chatting her head off. She had practically a full vocabulary by now, and joined in conversations with the odd swear word in between!

She loved this new adventure, having admiration and strokes from the crew members, along with a few nibbles of crisps and nuts. Happy as Larry, and she was a good traveller and enjoyed the flight and attention. She never knew until then that the 'love of her life' could fly too!

On arrival into Singapore, I waited for her to come through the quarantine area to be handed to me along with all her papers, and when she saw me as the cage was handed over it was, "Hello Mummy," and chat chat all the way home in the car.

As she entered the house with us, she saw through her cage the new house with loads of space, areas to fly around and sparkly things to chew. In addition, high ceilings that she could soar up to, before she dive-bombed down on to David's shoulder and squawked in a loud voice, "Oh wow!"

Yes, indeed, she was going to have a field day here! So, she was back in the hub of the family, flying freely around the house, and wrecking it bit by bit. Her favourite place was of course on David's shoulder. She had her favourite dressing gown – not hers, but her Daddy's! David would put it on for her when he got home, and she would perch on it for hours.

Together, they would sit in this attire, at the computer, in front of the television, or at the meal table, wrapped in their own little world! Needless to say, after a while the shoulders of this garment turned a completely different colour from the rest! At bedtime it was, "night night Daddy, night night Mummy, I love you," and in she went to the aviary in the back garden. Ah, peace!

One of the bedrooms I converted into a treatment room, and so little by little started up a clientele again, through friends and word of mouth. One of the treatments I included in my healing was aromatherapy. Aromatherapy was quite new to Singapore, and by chance at a party I met a guy who had a health food business and was interested in aromatherapy oils.

I had the idea of making my own aromatherapy remedies for my clients' ailments, and so joined him with my plan on board, to be partners. He was on the business side and I was on the public side. The next time I went to London to be with the children, I searched for my team and eventually found four professionals – a medical herbalist, a creative perfumer, a biologist and an aromatherapy chemist. It took a couple of years to get everything up and running, and then we launched and marketed them in Singapore in 1993 for the Asian market.

We had a selection of 30 mixes for insomnia, stress, colds, sinus problems, anxiety, fevers and rheumatism, to name a few. However, the most popular was the arthritis remedy, which we also formulated for horses. Very often I used these in conjunction with my healing to give it added benefits. The aromatherapy oils work through the olfactory system as well as the bloodstream via the skin.

I used to give talks all over Singapore, including at some of the top hotels where I placed my oils into their salons and spas. One of the best times I had was doing demos on horses in Kuala Lumpur. Charles was 16 and at home with us on holiday at this particular time, and he offered to come with me to KL and help me.

There was a big international show jumping event there, so without a thought, I had the idea to drive up there, fill the boot of the car with oils to sell, and then grab the odd horse before or after their competition to demonstrate a healing with the hope, of course, the owners would buy a bottle for themselves, if they wished. Anyway, it would be fun and we could stay in a hotel for a night and have more fun!

As we were driving to KL and chatting along the way, Charles said, "What's your plan when you get there?" "No idea, I shall just go by feel and play it by ear," I said. As we approached the Malaysian customs, we stopped and they wanted to look in the boot of the car.

"I hope you have papers for all the oils, Mummy," said Charles. "What papers?" I said. Oh, typical me, never even thought about it. Whoops, I shall be going off to the Malaysian jail now! Charles looked very worried, and the customs guy was asking me all sorts of questions, to most of which I replied no! I was talking too quickly, I think. "Well they are really just for demos etc. What's in them? Oh, the ingredients are on the back of the label. No, you don't drink it, no, nor do the horses. Didn't think I needed them. No, we haven't got papers. No, we don't live in KL. Car licence? Yes, I've got that," I said and gave him as big a smile as I could. Phew, he let us go through!

"That was a bit nerve-wracking," I said to Charles, "but sometimes you just have to go out on a limb. You never know what this adventure will lead to!" Mummy's words again, "Don't tell Daddy, he will think I'm an idiot," I said as I glanced at Charles as he tried to hide the smirk on his face.

Well yes, it did go well; Charles and I walked around the outside of the arena, and to where the horse lorries were, with horses being loaded and unloaded. We carried, or rather Charles carried, a box of oils and I chatted to passing horses and owners.

I spotted one horse that was very jumpy and obviously not comfortable in himself. I walked over to him and talked to him and his owner, having explained everything I did, and would do some healing on his horse if he wished, and use the oils for any aches or stiffness.

He accepted gladly and said that his horse was agitated and very stiff, and would not be able to compete well in the state he was in. Great, so this was the first treatment of the day. Yes, he bought a bottle of oil! But the best was that in no time the horse calmed down and soon was in the arena, calm and supple, performing a perfect clear round.

So, the day went on like this, and one horse fell asleep whilst I was doing him, and wanted to get down on the ground to sleep, and the swelling on his leg that I was treating had completely disappeared. I continued to do a few others with visible results, leaving with not many bottles of oils left to go through customs!

We were members at the polo club and went there often to have afternoon tea and watch the polo matches, and often in an evening, sundowners with friends and a meal. I frequently wandered around the stables and made friends with the polo ponies and chatted to the owners.

Patrick, owned by the club's manager and introduced to me by a guy I met in KL, was one of my favourite polo ponies. I often went to his stable and had a chat and a pat!

This particular day, he was competing in the home team, so it was very exciting to be able to watch him in action. I had been

A story of life-changing moments

treating Patrick on and off for some time now with a reoccurring back leg injury, but he seemed to be back on track and in great form for this special day.

The Rolex Cup match was great, with a win for the home team. Throughout the day, I had a few horses and riders brought to my side with bumps, kicks, strains and falls. For injured horses I took them to a nearby stable to administer healing, and for the riders, a first aid room in the club house. There was nothing so serious that 'hands-on healing' couldn't cope with.

At the end of the day, after the speeches, I was presented with a silver bracelet with a silver polo stick hanging from the chain, as thanks for my help with the wounded four-legged and two-legged players! It was a special gift which holds to this day those treasured memories.

A few months after the Rolex Cup, the club manager rang me to say that Patrick was in trouble, could I come immediately? Luckily, I was free and drove over in haste. Once I was in the stable with pony and owner, I was told that Patrick was in a bad way, and there was nothing that could be done for his injured leg. "He cannot play polo anymore and the advice was to have him shot," the manager said.

I was furious and said, "no way." I would come twice a week to give him healing, and for as long as it took. We were not going to give up on him.

The next series of events were one of the most bizarre happenings I have ever experienced in my field of work!

On my first day of healing Patrick, I was crouched down with my hands under his tummy to be able to reach the inside of his left rear leg where the injury was. He was very lame and obviously in quite a bit of pain. The club manager was with me throughout, and we were determined to do the best we could to get Patrick back on his feet and back on the polo fields that he loved so much.

The stable that we were in was alongside the polo fields and at the other side was virtually a jungle. The manager and I suddenly saw with amazement a wild cat speeding from there, across the polo fields towards us. As the cat approached our stable, the manager said that he had seen that cat many times, but no way would that feral cat come near any human being. Well, wrong! The cat flew into the open stable. I kept my healing position with hands on Patrick's injured leg. The cat ran up my back and sat on my shoulder and remained there in statue silence for the whole hour whilst I was doing my work. When I finished, he bolted out of the stable at speed to where he had come from.

We were speechless. The news of this happening spread around the club. On the next healing day, I had the club manager and the vet with me throughout the treatment. What! The same thing happened: the cat bolted in, ran up my back and sat as quiet as a mouse on my shoulder for, yet again, the whole treatment. After that, the cat ran as fast as he could back into the jungle.

On the next healing day, the manager came to watch, with the vet and the farrier. Oh my goodness! The same thing again! On the next healing day there came to watch one manager, one vet, one farrier, two club members and three children.

Oh gosh! Well, the next healing day? Yes, the same thing yet again. The cat was really on a mission. Our audience this time was one manager, one vet, one farrier, two club members, three children, and two newspaper reporters!

Isn't there a children's song that goes a bit like this? Anyway, after that we had crowds watching this amazing scene with the

A story of life-changing moments

cat climbing up my back and sitting on my shoulder for the whole treatment, in 'pin-dropping' silence until the hour was up.

Needless to say, Patrick was saved from the bullet, and his leg healed perfectly and he recovered to full health. He then continued with his passion of being a team member on the polo fields.

So the moral to this story is, yes, everyone can heal! In this case, the cat was my assistant. Cats and all other animals are healers too, and he took a major role in Patrick's healing. Thank you Cat. He knew what was happening, and instinctively knew what to do. After this event, Cat was never to be seen again. Mission accomplished. And yes, this is a true story!

"When I look into the eyes of an animal, I do not see an animal. I see a living being. I see a friend. I feel a soul."

- A.D. Williams

CHAPTER 12

SAY YES AND DO IT ANYWAY
How the Universe works its magic

I found that early mornings were my time to replenish my energies and what better way than to go for a long walk along the beach. The chorus of the birds, the sounds of nature, the smells, and up before the rest of the world is awake. 5am was the time I religiously flung myself out of the front door.

It was an amazing sight at the beach. Apart from the beauty and the stillness, many old people and some of a younger age would be in their groups, scattered along the grass lawns in front of the sea, doing their Tai Chi. They've got it right, I thought. Their dedication and discipline working with energies to keep themselves in good health, in both body and mind, was admirable.

I would sit in front of the sea, meditate and listen to the waves that were the only thing that broke the silence, in a soporific way! An hour or so later I would be back in the house and getting ready to go to the office for a busy non-stop day in the city. These precious hours were a must to start my day. It was during these special 'me' times I would get my ideas, map out my day's schedule, take a view of my life's mission and daydream!

One morning, I went to pick up some oils from the office to do some drop-offs to the hotels that had ordered them. At my first stop I bumped into the hotel manager and we had a chat. Through our conversation, he said to me, "The lady who has the contract for placing and managing the girls in the spa is leaving. Do you know of anyone who could take it over?"

Without even thinking, I said, "Yes, I can do that." What have I just said? I thought. Ah well, I am sure I can do it. Bit of a challenge though! He asked me if I had girls in mind to be able to replace the staff of five, trained in all treatments. "Yes," I said. The current girls were leaving in three months, so I had to get my girls ready for then. What girls?!

Excited and panicking a bit, I went back to the office and told my business partner what had happened. "Oh," he said, "can we do that?" "Yes, we can," I replied. "Let's get an advert in the local papers 'Masseurs wanted' and get cracking so that I can train them ready for the set date."

Can I do it, I thought, and then I remembered, yet again, Mummy's words: You can do anything you set your mind to. Just keep positive and push through the barrier of 'can't'. Well, I was already trained in all the treatments the spa was offering, so that's OK!

We had over 100 replies from the ad, and it was my task to interview them all. I ploughed through them all as quickly as I could and spent longer with the ones I thought had potential. I was horrified at some of the lives these candidates were having, from family and personal struggles to problems of immense gravity. I had masseurs, beauty therapists, reflexologists, ex-prostitutes, transvestites, plus other therapists. It was an eye-opening experience!

A story of life-changing moments

From the second round of interviews, I took on five girls that I really liked, felt I could trust, and be able to help change their lives for the better. All the others needed help, so I kept a list of the possible candidates for a later date.

Now I had the task of training them up with all the treatments that the spa offered. Quite easy really, as they were all keen to have good jobs, and they had the basic skills already. Most of them were natural masseuses, as it was quite common in Asia that mothers would hand down their knowledge and teach their daughters how to massage from an early age.

The girls were then placed into the hotel and they proved to be a great success. From the reputation we positively built there, the other hotels heard what I was doing, and in not too long a time I had eight top hotels in Singapore and one at Changi airport. In all I had 40 girls who I took care of and mentored throughout my seven remaining years in Singapore.

Some of these girls' stories were heartbreaking and I wanted to make sure that they were treated well, like family, and were paid a decent salary. Many an evening I would have a phone call from one of them with a situation or problem they couldn't handle, and I would listen and help them as much as I could. I wanted to make a difference to their lives, and give them my support. At Christmas time, I would give them a party, which would be at a venue of their choice. Their favourite one was out on a boat for dinner and dancing, along with karaoke, which they all loved. I dreaded how they would always pull me up on stage to sing. But it made them laugh so much as I am tone deaf and sing totally out of tune! Ghastly!

When I eventually left the country, I was very sad to leave these lovely girls. All 40 of them had been loyal to me throughout this time. Their lives had certainly changed from their shaky start when I first met them to confident girls with self-respect and a purpose in life. Bless them.

When the 10 years had gone by, we were ready to leave Singapore and David was going to take a position flying from the Singapore Airlines base in London. At this time, we decided to search for a house in France. The children had grown up and both were with their respective girlfriend and boyfriend. Where did that time go?

"A gentle word, a kind look, a good-natured smile can work wonders and accomplish miracles."

- William Hazlitt

CHAPTER 13

MOISSAC, FRANCE

Having to heal myself as well as others

France. Yes! Really getting excited. After a lot of looking around we found an amazing house just outside Moissac, about an hour from Toulouse. I can't say that David was very thrilled with it as it was very old and a bit tired; a home full of character, which was my thing, and full of problems, which wasn't his! However, time was running out for getting back to Singapore, so we took the plunge!

The situation was a dream, on a hill which offered an amazing view of the Pyrenees and roaming countryside. We had around three acres of garden including orchards of apples and plums, alongside a long stretch of grass which lent itself for a golf practice area. The children would love that when they came out for their holidays!

The house was an old converted barn, with four bedrooms downstairs, a long hallway leading to a steep staircase going up to the open-plan dining room a level above, alongside a sunken lounge. The American kitchen, with a bar overlooking the French windows, led to a large entertaining balcony.

From the dining area there was a staircase leading to a minstrel's gallery with a library section adjoined. In addition, there was another little staircase at the end of the dining area to another bedroom, which was perfect in size to accommodate our four-poster bed, and from there down some little steps to an open-plan bathroom. The whole of the upper floor had beautiful wooden beams throughout with many spiders enjoying their home in their intricate webs spun from beam to beam!

So out came all our crates from storage in the UK, which was massive, but all fitted in perfectly actually, albeit I threw quite a bit out, wondering why on earth I had kept things like Vicky's plaster that she had had on her broken leg, covered in signatures from her friends at school! Now it was like a crushed meringue scattering crumbs all over the floor.

When all the furniture was in place, we had a wonderful fusion of styles with Middle Eastern, Asian, and heirloom antiques. Stunning. I was settling in as fast as I could, and at this time David was away a lot. Most of the time I was on my own, with no friends except 'here we go again' footsteps walking back and forth along the downstairs corridors throughout the night. I never ever saw anyone, but always heard the footsteps, as did some of my guests. He must be guarding over me, I thought, as I felt comfortable with him there.

Not long after I was living in my 'little piece of Heaven' I had a call from my cousin in Brussels who was in a very bad way with cancer, and he asked me to go over to be with him and his girlfriend, to help him. They had both been over to Singapore for a holiday not so long ago, and he had seen what I had been doing with healing and helping people. It was really a last hope, last resort for him. He wanted peace of mind and to come out of the fear of dying. He was a lovely guy about 10 years younger than me, and had a great sense of humour, and we always got on like a house on fire and laughed a lot. When I got there, I was

A story of life-changing moments

shocked to see how bad he was, and straight away set up a room at the top of the house for healing and meditation.

I went off to town as soon as I could to buy crystals, candles and CDs to make our little sanctuary special for him. I set out to do a two-week programme for him, which we did every day for near enough the whole day, along with his partner joining us for some of his sessions.

Here we had peace, and we did healings twice a day, and a lot of meditating and talking throughout. We knew that physically there was not a lot could be done, bar ease the pain and quieten the mind. However, the joy of being with each other and laughing a lot, with the unconditional love of a family member, was so precious, and we felt that bond.

On one meditation, I took him to our favourite place on the beach, where we sat beside each other on a bench. Here we had the intention to meet our fathers who had already gone many years ago and to speak with them along with our guardian angels. When we finished the session, we shared our experiences and found out that we more or less had visions and conversations that matched. It was a very comforting experience of love and peace.

We repeated that exercise many times over the time I was there, and finally he was coming out of fear. After I came home, a couple of weeks later, I had a call from my cousin's partner to say that he was now in hospital and it wouldn't be long. She had called in a priest and he was going to perform the marriage vows at his bedside, as they wished for her to carry his name on to represent the great love that they had together on earth.

A couple of days after that, he went off in peace, with his newly-wedded wife by his side, clutching a little angel that I gave him a long time ago, with the feeling that I was also with him in spirit.

The funeral in Scotland was beautiful; the family thanked me for my help, which they said was invaluable, but actually for me it was an honour to be with him at this transient time.

I have been with a few friends as they have crossed over, and it is always a privilege for that soul to have you there at that time of passing. The soul always chooses who they want to be with them at the end.

Very often there is guilt from a loved one who wasn't able to be there at that time. However, you could remain in that room 24/7 and then pop out for a coffee, to return too late. For whatever reason, and sometimes the best for the waiting member, that particular soul has chosen for it to be that way.

When people need my help, they are put in front of me. There are never any coincidences. I knew that people would come across my path for help but here, in France, I had no friends as yet, and I was in the middle of nowhere, with only the sheep, cows, and dogs yapping at night on the hill behind the house.

I found a lovely restaurant in Moissac that did all of my favourite French dishes. As I wanted to get out and meet people, I decided that I would go there for dinner regularly, and maybe I would meet the locals, English people and make friends!

Well it didn't work, everyone sat in couples, or in groups, and I just blended into the background. The owner of the restaurant, Jean Pierre, was a burly chatty, or 'chat up' I should say, Frenchman! He didn't speak English, so that was a bonus to be able to practise my French.

He was actually very kind to me and helped me find workmen, like electricians when the lights went out, or plumbers when there was a water leak etc., and there was always a free glass of wine ready for me on my table each time I visited! One evening when I was down in the town having dinner and watching the couples alongside me chatting, laughing and enjoying themselves, I had an idea. Let's have a go!

At the end of dinner, and ready to leave, I paid my bill and said to Jean Pierre, "You know that English couple that have just left, the lady with the blonde hair and the handsome husband? They look very nice, do you have their telephone number, if so, could I have it please?" "Oh OK, yes I do, let me get it for you," he said and promptly went off to find it.

The next day, I rang the number and spoke with the lady. "You don't know me, but I saw you in Jean Pierre's restaurant last night. I am new here, and I am looking for friends, and wondered if you would both like to come over for a drink." I said it very quickly so that I wouldn't lose my nerve! "Yes, why not," she replied, and that was the start of my friends collection.

I did a few more rounds of collecting numbers at the restaurant and with the same speech making telephone calls the following day. Within a few weeks I had collected around 40 new friends through calling like this, and made friends with their friends too. Friends through the calls, and friends of those, now new friends. It was amazing and my social life started to flourish.

Here again I set up a healing room in the house, and gradually I had regulars of those friends, and others, coming for sessions. This home was also a sanctuary for myself. Little by little, David stayed away more, and then after a year or so, he decided to take the Singapore posting back as he hated it in Moissac.

I felt that we were in trouble, and I was in fear of the outcome. I threw myself back into my paintings for therapy, meditated a lot and asked my angels for help. I felt that I was losing myself, let alone him. Never mind helping everyone else, I needed to help me! What was I doing here alone?

We soldiered on for a while and then we were on the move again. This time it was home, back to Moy Lodge, our family home that I loved and where the children were very happy.

"You don't have to have it all figured out to move forward."

www.powerofpositivity.com

A story of life-changing moments

CHAPTER 14

RETURNING HOME
Meeting my guardian angel

When we got back to the UK, things seemed to be looking up for us, and we decided to renovate the house from top to bottom.

Painting throughout, new curtains, en suite bathrooms installed, the lot. It was a sight to be seen in *Homes and Gardens* for sure. By the time we finished, Vicky was about to get married, Charles's first son was about to be born, our marriage broke down, and David and I were about to divorce.

Divorcing was one of the worst times in my life. I hibernated for a long time, to try and pick up the pieces of 'me'. Vicky scooped me up and took me to her place with her new husband for a couple of weeks. Over that time, I had total memory blanks. It felt like it was the end of the world, and I sat on the floor of my bedroom crying for hours. I was a complete zombie.

My children were amazing and fully supportive, and reassured me that I would be OK. I didn't feel it; I was in a wilderness period, of being totally lost and frightened. I knew I had to get myself up and back on track, yup, get up and get on. I need to take my power back. I will be fine!

It is exceedingly tough, as anyone who has been through this knows, and been in this black hole. There is always light after the darkness, and we just have to trust and believe that all will be right at the end of the day. But we also have to help ourselves. I decided to have some time away, so rang Jill, a very good girlfriend of mine in Geneva, and told her how bad I was feeling and needed a break. She immediately said, "Get on the plane and come and stay with us for a while, as long as you like."

Off I went, and one day Jill and I were sitting in the kitchen chatting about what my plan was now. "I have to get back to work," I said, and asked her if she knew of any clinic in Geneva that would be interested in my work.

"Oh," she said, "I think there is a 'spooks' place just down the road from here, shall we go and have a look at it?" Jill always used to say that my work was spooky, and was always amazed when the clients turned around for the better and healed. We always laughed about it, and actually still do.

I thought it would be a good idea to work occasionally abroad, so I was up for it. Jill and I duly arrived at the centre and walked in and asked the receptionist if we could see the owner. She seemed a bit busy but waved us over to the seating area to wait. "Yes, yes please take a seat, she won't be long!"

Funny thing to say, well anyway we settled down. A few minutes later a lady came out of her office, looked at me, and said, "Please do come in." We introduced ourselves, and then she asked me to sit down and tell me about all that I did, and then give her a short sample treatment.

Following that, she said, "Yes I think it would be great to have you here. Shall we give it a trial of 10 days and then go from there?"

Wow, that was quick. So that was the start of my nine years in this clinic. After the initial trial, I started with one full week a year and built up to two weeks three times a year! We were full most of the time, and then I started creating Angel Workshops with all the tools that I use. These too became popular.

After a couple of years when Isabel and I became really good friends, and we were having dinner together, she said, "I have a secret to tell you. When you came to see me in my office the first time, I thought you were the lady I was expecting that did hypnotherapy, and when you sat down, I was beginning to realise that you were not her. The receptionist obviously assumed you were, and just sat you down in the chairs outside my office. I got really interested in what you were saying, and I liked you, so that made my mind up immediately." No coincidence!

I will never forget the kindness of Jill, and the way she helped me. I have a lot to thank her for. She helped me pick up the pieces of me, and stood by me all these years. She helped to launch me into Switzerland. I stayed with her for many years whilst I was in Isabel's clinic and she looked after me as family. I don't know what I would have done without her.

I was certainly well in tune with my angels by now and the Angel Workshop was a wonderful and enlightening day for my participants, and for myself. I wanted to share as much of my knowledge and experience with everyone. We have many angels working for us, but we have to ask them for help when we need it. We all carry on with our lives, and at times of struggle it is great to get their help.

The Angel Workshop is a day of sharing, helping each other and gathering knowledge. It is all about feelings and feeling the energies. When you ask for help from the angels, they are straight away on the job to bring to you what you are asking for, as long as it is for your highest good!

Of course, you have to be polite and remember to say please and thank you! When your question has been put out to them, a few days later they will present to you a white feather, which will be just one, in an unusual place, like on the kitchen table, the floor of the sitting room, on the bonnet of your car, or even floating down from the sky in front of your eyes.

Pick it up and say thank you angels. This is their sign to say that they are on the job. Then gradually you will see little miracles happening in your life that are bringing you nearer and nearer to the answer to your prayers.

Throughout the day, we do many meditations to clear ourselves of toxins and stress, aligning us with the higher energies. Once we are in these energies, we will hear or sense answers related to our questions that we have put up. There is a very potent angelic mantra we use many times between meditations and exercises. It is an angel invocation, and you can actually feel the energies getting higher and higher. Anyone sensitive to energy will feel or perhaps see angels flocking in from everywhere to be with them.

This simple little chant is another way to use sounds your body makes to align with the angels. There are only four words to it, three of which are repeated three times, and then one that you say once to end it. You can repeat the chant as many times as you like. Each word is chanted with the same sound. You can use any note that feels right to you. Experiment with it until you find a note that feels clear and comfortable. Here are the words:

Eee Nu Rah

Eee Nu Rah

A story of life-changing moments

Eee Nu Rah

Zay

Eee means 'all that I am that is not physical, my mind and my emotions'

Nu means 'my physical body'

Rah means 'my soul'

Zay means 'in the company of angels'

Together the words of the chant say 'I bring all of myself, mind, emotions, body and soul, together in the company of the angels.'

This is a quick and easy way to invoke the angels – a way of saying 'angels, here I am ready to be with you'. It's simple. It works. Give it a 'chants'! By the end of the day, we all get the names of our guardian angels, which are not necessarily biblical names. One of my first workshops I held, I got my own guardian angel's name, which is George, and this story I share with my group. It was one of the most incredible things that ever happened to me in my life.

It had been a couple years after leaving Singapore when I received an email from a centre there, asking me over to do a couple of weeks' healing. I thought great, I would love to return for a visit and catch up with some friends, and so accepted.

Getting excited to be back again, I duly arrived at the centre, which I actually had never been to before. Well, it was a bit basic, and as soon as I was in and settled, I really didn't like the feeling I was having. Intuition was saying 'get me out of here!' Too right, I had a number of difficult clients who certainly were coming to the wrong person for their needs.

The last straw was with guys coming in saying, "Can you please take this black magic or voodoo spell on me?" or put one on someone they wanted to revenge. Not my job. "There is black gunge coming out through my stomach, would you like to see it?" No thank you. "I have someone that is after me to murder me." Go to the police.

Then a poor lady came in, totally out of her mind literally, who should have been in a psychiatric hospital. She had probably been hidden away at home by her family, so as not to lose face by taking her to the appropriate mental hospital! Oh my goodness, I thought, I want to go home!

On the plane going home, I thought that's it, I am going to give it all up, can't be dealing with people being put in front of me with these kinds of conditions. Well, I only had a few days back home, and then I was going on to Spain to stay with a girlfriend who was bringing in a number of people for me to help. I couldn't let her down, but after that, that's it!

So, there I was at Heathrow airport again and my gate for Palma was called. Off I went into the boarding lounge. There weren't many people around, so I sat in a row of seats to myself.

I had the strangest feeling that something was about to happen, and suddenly from the corner of my eye I saw a figure coming towards me. I did a double take as this didn't seem to be any ordinary guy. He wasn't just walking towards me; he was gliding along the floor. Drop dead gorgeous black man, well over six feet and impeccably dressed, in a long cashmere coat, carrying a briefcase and a mobile phone to his ear.

I knew he was going to sit down beside me, even although there were plenty of seats free. I felt prickles go up my spine. I thought he is going to give me a message of some kind, I just know it.

Yup, down he sat in the seat beside me, with empty seats either side of us. What on earth was he going to say? Well nothing actually, as our flight was called and boarding had started. Oh well, so much for my intuition, so I stood up and walked towards the gate.

I entered the plane and found my aisle seat, put my cabin bag in the overhead locker and sat down. A few minutes later this guy was gliding down the aisle towards me. I couldn't understand why everyone else wasn't looking at him, as he stood out with his amazing presence, and was almost walking on air! I just knew he was going to sit beside me this time!

As he came near to me, he gave me a beaming smile, passed me and continued to glide down the cabin. Oh that's it then? No, not at all, after a couple of minutes he returned to a couple of rows in front of me, then turned around and back he came, pointing to the window seat in my row, and said to me, "excuse me, I think that's my seat."

Once he had settled, and after a few minutes, with no introduction he said to me, "In other lives, I too have seen those that do black magic and voodoo, and now I am here to help you with your important work as a healer. You can't give it up. You have your life purpose, and I am here to give you this message." He then continued to tell me all that I had been doing, and how important it was for me to carry on with my mission.

I was absolutely speechless. He was accurate to every detail of what I was doing. I actually wondered if he was real. I thought what happens when the stewardess gives him coffee, will it go right through him, or if I touch his sleeve, will he actually be there? No, he accepted a coffee and it stayed in his body!

We walked off the plane together, and I was dying to go to the loo, so excused myself. He said, "I will see you at the other side of passport control." You've got to be joking, I thought, as I looked at the queue, it is going to take forever. Anyway, off I went, and when I came back the queues were huge, but there he was, waiting at the other side. How did he do that?

Once I eventually caught up with him, we walked outside the building together. I had already told him that I had a lift coming and he had his car parked in the car park.

Standing together, I thanked him and told him my name. He replied, "I know. Mine is George." Whilst saying our goodbyes, I heard a car approaching and turned my head to see if it was mine, which it wasn't, then swiftly back. He had totally disappeared. There was no way that he could have gone out of sight that quickly. Thank you George. It was my guardian angel.

Very often divine intervention can take place and an angel can be disguised in a human body. Often you hear of cases when, say, a child is crossing a busy road in front of a speeding car and is scooped up quickly by a person and carried off to safety. Later that child would say that it was someone he or she recognised, a grandparent maybe, or someone they knew that had moved on.

In the workshops we also do intuition work and healing, which is certainly very effective with the collective energies of a group. There are many tools that one can use, and visualisation is one of the strongest. This is one of the best I give to everyone.

When you are under the shower each morning, visualise the water a bright blue colour, and instead of going over you, it is going through you from the top of your head and all the way down to your feet.

As this healing blue liquid is passing through your body, stop at the parts where you think you need help, and swirl it around there for a bit longer. Then it continues to go down, through

A story of life-changing moments

your torso, legs and feet. As it comes out of your feet, it turns brown in colour and runs into the drain, as you visualise all your toxins, sickness and negativity coming out of your body and flushing away.

I use this blue liquid visualisation in many ways when I am doing my healing, either visualising injections of blue healing liquid going into the parts that need help, or visualising it swirling around the affected area.

This particular time, I was in the UK, and I had been asked to go and give a healing demonstration on horses in Wales. When I arrived at the yard, there were many riders and owners waiting for me, sitting on bales of straw, hanging around, chatting and waiting for me to start.

First of all, I did an introductory talk on my background and what I do and what I was going to do! Questions were coming out before I started, and I felt I had quite a few sceptics here! So I said to the angels, please help me with this lot, and please give me an easy horse, with a problem that is simple to get to, and not under his tummy where I have to be a contortionist to get to it, and having to speak up, explaining what I am doing at the same time!

Out came an unknown horse to me, very lame, and hobbled across to where I was standing, led by his owner. Ah that's easy, I thought, it's a front leg, or actually a hoof as he has a bandage on it. I shan't be crawling under him! The first thing I have to do is go into his head, to see where he is at and any past traumas he may have gone through.

To start with, I tuned in with him, and as usual I incorporated EFT (Emotional Freedom Techniques), which is used to get the feeling of traumas out of his body. This was easy, as he had a lovely owner and was perfectly happy where he was. He had just the one owner and was very bonded with her. As I put my hands on him, I was guided to the parts that needed help, but this time it was obvious anyway.

As the owner took the bandage off and I started my healing procedure, I then talked the audience through everything. Here the underside of his hoof was infected, swollen and painful. So, I put the intention up to what needed healing, asked the angels for help, and then just kept my hands over it. I felt the heat coming through the palms of my hands, and just knew it was going to work. I then did a visualisation of injections of blue healing liquid going into the affected area. After around an hour, I had finished and the hoof was re-bandaged, and the horse was led back to the stable.

The following morning, I went back to the yard, with several of the audience that were with me for the demo the day before, especially the sceptics, to see if there was an improvement.

We went to his stable and the owner took the bandages off his hoof, and as the bandages came off, they were sodden with blue liquid, and the inside of his underfoot had greatly improved. Sometimes, but not often, a manifestation takes place, as it did this time. Aghast, the sceptics no longer were! Thank you again to the angels, little miracles do happen.

Katherine had a mare that just couldn't get pregnant, and she asked me if I could help her, so I went along and did a rebalancing healing on her, and it was only the once. Not long after that, the mare fell pregnant with twins! Unfortunately, with horses, they can only deliver one, so the other had to be taken away. After the remaining foal was born, I had the privilege of being with it for quality time, with it falling asleep whilst I was giving it a general healing, and it lying down on the ground whilst I finished the treatment. Magic!

I was now working a lot with animals when I was in the UK, which I loved, especially the horses, which were my passion, when Suzie, a very good friend of mine who lived in Hastings, called me in a total panic saying that her young golden Labrador, Mr Jones, was in trouble. She had taken him to the vet and he had an enlarged heart and she was told he would not survive the night. His heart was a staggering 350 per minute and his blood pressure was barely readable because it was so low.

I didn't think twice about going as quickly as I could, made a few phone calls to cancel a few days' appointments, threw some things into my suitcase, and in haste drove off to Hastings. When I arrived, Suzie was so pleased to see me. I said I would start working straight away. In fact, I stayed one week, and there wasn't a waking moment that I didn't have my hands on Mr Jones, apart from meal times of course, but that was all. He sat beside me all the time whilst he was having his healing, and I just knew he knew what I was doing. As I have said before, animals accept healing automatically, with total trust and knowing.

After concentrated quality time with him, I returned home. The following day after my visit, Suzie took Mr Jones back to the vets for an x-ray and ultrasound. His heart was back to normal size, and the vet was amazed. He was still on drugs of course and those he certainly had to have.

Six months later when she went back to the vet for his check-up, Suzie was concerned about the vet saying they would reduce his medication. However, the vet explained that a special blood test could determine if the drugs were keeping him going or if his heart was functioning correctly. When the results of the blood tests came back, they proved that Mr Jones's heart was working for itself! The vets in the practice were amazed at his recovery.

Suzie was over the moon. I was thrilled that I was able to give a helping hand alongside the vets. Good team work. He has now just had his eighth birthday and is still a puppy at heart!

"Angels come to help and guide us in as many guises as there are people who need their assistance."

- Eileen Elias Freeman

CHAPTER 15

GREEN OF ANGELS
Surrounded by angels and receiving their help

I had left Moy Lodge and had to be carried out of there kicking and screaming! Well not quite, but the parting was terrible. The house hunting prior to that was a nightmare, there was nothing that I could find in the price bracket I had, or even remotely like it, when a friend rang me and said that she had seen a place in the newspaper that would suit me down to the ground and she gave me the details. "It's in Englefield Green," she said. "Where on earth is that?" I said, "Never heard of it."

When I went for the viewing – it was perfect. Well, it needed a lot doing, but I had the vision. It was very tired looking but had a lovely faded elegance. It was an apartment on the first floor of a Georgian building in a perfect situation, quite near to Heathrow airport and not far from London, in a little 'village with a green' of typical English character.

As you walked in, the first thing you saw was the 'wow factor' of a high ceiling, ornate in blue and white cornicing of that period. Then there was a large drawing room through the dining room and entrance, and two big bedrooms, dining area, and a balcony stretching from the drawing room to my bedroom. The balcony was derelict really, bare slated floor surface and totally empty. However, the vision I had for that would restore it to perfection, as with the rest of my new home.

The sale of Moy Lodge had fallen through and I had already put in an offer for the apartment, so I had to pull out, but I had hope and kept positive that the apartment would wait for me. If it was meant for me, I just knew it would happen. I was madly asking my angels to keep my perfect home for me, when six months later my dream came true.

All the furniture that I had taken with me, with all the memories from all the countries we had lived in, actually fitted in perfectly without an inch to spare. Even the four-poster bed, which was a must, took precedence in my bedroom, with all my favourite soft toys on top of it! Was it cluttered? No! Full of history, with a fusion of mix and match everything! Character? Full of it! I repaired the balcony, decorated it with lots of pots and plants, small tables and chairs, and hanging baskets over the wooden balcony rails. Perfect! I had the apartment painted throughout, plus a new carpet laid, put in fitted wardrobes in my bedroom, and the spare bedroom doubled up as a guest room and treatment room. Done. Electricity not perfect, plumbing not perfect, but I would deal with that later!

After a number of years, a friend of mine said, "Just 'you' this place, isn't it, with the name Englefield Green?" "What do you mean?" I replied? "Well, Englefield Green of course, Green of Angels!" "Oh," the penny dropped. How come I didn't click on to that one? Yes, indeed, and I was convinced I was brought here by the angels. Yet again, no coincidence!

This time, when I was in Geneva, Paul came to me after he had had a nasty climbing accident and tore his Achilles tendon. The tendon was completely severed, resulting in a 7mm gap between the ends. Reconnecting the tendon required surgery, which was

A story of life-changing moments

completed a week later. With his leg in plaster and needing crutches for six weeks, he was told not to put pressure on it for two weeks after the plaster was taken off.

It was then when the plaster had been taken off that he came to me. He was very sceptical, but his wife had said to him that she had seen this healer and said it would do him good anyway, and you never know what might happen!

I explained to him what I was doing – that I would just be putting my hands on the injury and he would feel the heat. I also explained that the healing would continue after he left me. At the end of the session, I said I felt it would heal very quickly. "Great," he said.

When he came back the next time, he said that after 10 days he felt tingling sensations in the tendon, and he knew instinctively that it was the result of the healing, and that it would make a big difference to his recovery. Two weeks later he went back to the doctor for a check-up, and the doctor was amazed at the flexibility of his ankle and tendon, plus the fact that he could raise his heel off the floor so early in the recovery process.

In between doctor's appointments Paul came back to me for top-ups, and told me of the speed of his recovery. Then the final time he was with me, he said that at his last appointment with the doctor he was doing toe-raises and balancing on the toes of his foot. The doctor was completely amazed and said to him, "I have never seen anyone recover so quickly from this type of surgery. You must be in the 99th percentile." Paul replied, "Yes I know!"

All of the check-ups, x-rays and ultrasounds showed that the tendon was fully recovered within nine weeks of the plaster being removed (normally it takes five to six months). He even returned to climbing. His friends thought he was crazy to do it so quickly. But he knew it wouldn't be a problem, and it wasn't.

Very often I get called out to sick horses that are miles away and in the middle of nowhere. This time it was in Sussex and the yard was in the grounds of an old abbey. Sometimes, annoyingly, the sat nav goes out of range, and it can be like a treasure hunt of landmark clues given to me by the owners for the directions. This was no exception.

I had met Pippa in London at a social event, and we got talking about her two horses, Ted and Walter. Through the conversation, I just had a feeling that there was an urgency for me to see Ted, but I couldn't put a finger on it, I just knew that I had to go.

When I eventually arrived, the yard was quite large, and Ted and Walter's stables were separated from the rest of the horses, and sat on their own. They were devoted to each other, and it was great that they shared their accommodation with just themselves.

To start, when I met them, I spent some time chatting and getting to know their individual personalities, and surprising Pippa when I said that Walter liked to be a trouble maker and enjoyed clowning around! Which was absolutely true. The two horses were inseparable and hated being apart. Health-wise Walter was fine; it was Ted that I was anxious about.

Pippa told me that Ted, the pony, had been becoming increasingly unwell with an ailment that the vet so far had been unable to help him with. He had just recovered from a very bad bout of laminitis, and since slowly returning to his paddock he had suffered with exceptionally swollen 'grass glands', to the point his glands were so swollen that his breathing was very laboured and showed no sign of returning to normal.

Ted was a beautiful grey pony with a beautiful nature. He was very sensitive to energies and therefore very receptive. At this point, I didn't know all of Ted's history, so I moved in to feel what I could find, and scan him all over. Then I would pick up where I needed to spend more time on the healing.

As soon as I put my hands on him to see where the problems were, I was drawn straight to the aches he felt from his sacroiliac. Then I was drawn to the hoof that I found out later had nearly suffered a full pedal bone rotation earlier in the year. Moving on, I went to his neck and worked for quite some time on the swollen glands and, seeing that his breathing was very laboured, did some more.

Pippa and I were quite concerned watching him struggle for breath, when all of a sudden, he gave a large cough, and with a look in his eyes of thanks, his breathing came back to normal. We couldn't believe our eyes. Well I could, thank you angels.

He was fine for a few months until I got a call from Pippa to come back as his breathing was bad again. This time I said to her that I felt large blocks in his neck, and to get the vet out as soon as possible. She did so, that night, and Ted was admitted to the Royal Veterinary Clinic.

Here a CT scan identified what the vets believed to be an enormous tumour restricting his trachea as well as putting some pressure on his vertebrae. The size of the tumour meant that removal would be too risky and so it was decided that Ted would be sent out with a permanent tracheotomy to live out his final weeks/months until the benign tumour grew to an unmanageable size.

When I got the news of him coming home, I decided to be there for his arrival. Then I would give Ted a treatment to help his healing process. It was so wonderful to see the reunion of Ted and Walter, they were nose to nose, grooming each other with the delight and prancing around the paddock.

When we took Ted into his stable for a treatment, I knew he was pleased to see me, and he readily settled down for a healing treatment. My aim was to see if we could break down the tumour so that it would disappear. I could sense little gravelly bits breaking up and was praying that we could do it. A big ask! But I knew that the healing and help would be coming through me!

A few days later Pippa sent me a photo. "Look at this," she wrote. It was a photo of Ted in his stable. He was very happy, great that's good news, I thought. Then there was another picture with words written on it.

"I came into Ted's stable this morning and saw that the stable door was coated in a thick porridge-like substance that had sprayed out of his tracheotomy hole!" Here was the picture of the stable door, and it was well and truly covered with a gungy mass.

For the next few days the substance continued to drain from his tracheotomy hole. Over the course of a few weeks the 'tumour' all but disappeared, and Ted found himself back out in the field gaining condition and finding a new lease of life. Years later, the pony that had only a few weeks to live is still going strong and the lumps around his neck are almost non-existent.

I have a very dear friend of mine called Heather, from our Bahrain days who also lives in the UK now, not far from me, and we often get together and reminisce on the old days!

Her home, which is set in beautiful grounds with a lake, is perfect for entertaining, and many parties with friends from around the world have brought us all together here over the

A story of life-changing moments

years. In the summer, the parties were held in the stunning grounds and there would be tables laden with mouth-watering food in abundance. And yes, you're right, it has been known on occasions that over excited, over the limit guests have fallen into the lake, escaping luckily with only hurt pride!

One day Heather rang me to ask for my help. Actually, it wasn't for her but for one of the local guys, who was passionate about fishing and enjoyed coming on occasion to see her and enjoy a day at the lake. He was in his thirties and had just been diagnosed with a brain tumour. There was nothing that could be done and it was a last hope, to ask me to help him in any way I could. Of course, I would, and said I would be over the next day.

When I arrived, Heather was waiting for me and off we went to the lake side to find Luis. What a lovely guy, charming, great sense of humour and well mannered. We chatted away for a long time about everything and nothing, I then explained to him what I do, and said to him, "Do you believe in angels?" "I think so," he replied. We then continued to talk about angels, his guardian angel and how they helped everyone, how they listened to you, talked to you, and were always around you.

"Did you know that angels present you with white feathers, real ones, when they are around you and helping you with what you are asking for?" I said. "No," he said. "Oh, OK, well they do," I replied. "May I give you a healing? It will help you to feel better." "OK," he said, "where shall we do it?" "Here," I said. "This is your favourite place and it is a nice hot day. We will do it on the grass at the side of the lake."

So that's exactly what we did. He lay outstretched on the grass with a coat for a pillow under his head. We enjoyed being out in the grounds, with the sun shining down on us, with all nature's colours, sounds, and the universal energies around us. He felt better in himself after that, and felt calm and at peace.

I gave him one of my little angel stones to keep with him when he was connecting to the angels to give him strength, with the promise that I would come back each week to repeat the session and have a chat. He was so pleased to know that I was there to help him as much as I could.

We had many times together, repeating the same healings, and lovely long chats on the grass by the lake. During our sessions he used to say, "This is my little piece of Heaven here, and if I have to go, this would be the place I would like to be."

Many weeks afterwards, I had a call from Heather crying hysterically, saying that she had just been out to the lake to give Luis a coffee, and saw him upside down floating in the lake, obviously been there for a long time, and was dead. Would I come over straight away to be with her? The police, medics, and others were on their way. Of course, I was in the car like a flash.

When I arrived, the police were at the gates and no one was allowed in. The tapes were across the road and driveway. "Heather wants me with her, ring her and then let me in please," I said. I went in as soon as the police officer came off the phone. Heather was distraught in the kitchen where I found her, and not long after that the body was being taken out of the lake.

After a while the officer was asking us questions, along with another officer who had joined us. We walked with them around the edge of the lake to see if there was any evidence of a fall or trip into the lake from the grass verges. No, not that we could see so far. Then suddenly, further around the lake, on the grass near the edge, was a huge circle of hundreds of white feathers!

A story of life-changing moments

Heather and I looked at each other in amazement and knew that the angels had given him his wish of leaving us, here, in his 'little piece of Heaven'. We turned around to the officers and said it was here that he went in. "How do you know?" the male officer said. The female officer answered, "It must be here, it is circled with white feathers, that's the presence of angels!"

Heather and I were aghast that the female officer had also given us confirmation, and directly after that we saw a large fish jump out of the water, then it dived straight back in! Another sign! Luis was at peace, and we knew it was the right place for him to choose to go. The male officer thought we were nuts; however, we did have a swift chat afterwards with the female officer about angels!

I still keep in touch with Luis's family, and from time to time we see each other and talk about him with fond memories and the angels.

A quote from his family:
"Our angels symbolise hope and offer a beacon of light in otherwise trying or difficult times."

CHAPTER 16

EMERGENCIES
Being in the right place at the right time

I knew for a long time that I would be working in Dubai but I didn't know the 'how and when'! I had been visualising me working there and asking my angels to work out the logistics etc. Then it actually happened.

A few years ago, a great friend of mine, who I also knew in the days we all lived in Bahrain, was now living in Dubai. Susan was staying with Heather for a while when I invited them over. They both came to me for a meal, and I offered them each a rebalancing healing treatment as they were tired and a bit stressed out with their work.

Afterwards, as we girls do, we chatted about everything and Susan said, "I think you should come and do some work in Dubai, you can stay with me and I will help you." Two words from me, "Yes please," and another two, "Thank you."

So that was it, and I was so excited, dates organised, and off I went. Now a few years behind me, it is one of my favourite places. One of the stories which is very memorable was during one of my sessions with a lady who was pregnant and had a couple of weeks to go.

This was her first baby and she was hoping to have a quick labour, and was really anxious that it would be a long one. She was really ready to have it now, she was very uncomfortable, and wanted it now! "It won't be long, sooner than you think, don't worry," I said, and we talked about angels and how to work with them. "I really want to know more about angels," she said. I was doing an Angel Workshop in a couple of days so invited her along. "Perfect," she said, "perfect timing as I am not due yet."

We had 10 participants at the workshop, and it was a great group. As always happens, we are like a family and support each other with everything, and normally little miracles happen on that day!

The energies were very high and we could feel them. Near the end, we were sitting in a circle and I was giving our last meditation to the group. Whilst delivering the words, I looked up as the mother-to-be excused herself and ran off. A few minutes later she came back with a towel in her hands, then sat on it and continued the meditation with us. Oh, she must be uncomfortable, I thought.

When everyone opened their eyes, the mother-to-be announced that her waters had broken, and maybe she should go to hospital? "Yes," we all said in unison. She was in no hurry, said her goodbyes, and wanted to drive herself. In fact, she was going to go home for her husband first. "No panic," she said, "we are in the hands of angels!"

It was the end of the workshop anyway, and we were all thrilled for her. That was quicker than she thought! She did actually get in her car as her home was just around the corner, with an escort of two of the participants who had now got their wings! Within

A story of life-changing moments

just a few hours she gave birth to a little angel. It was her wish, a little girl.

Being in the right time and the right place, they say! Not a coincidence, they say! Absolutely! Ain't that the truth! When some people need help, and there is no one there for them, then what? A chance meeting with a person offering a helping hand?

I was particularly busy with clients over this day, and all I needed was a trip to London, for an urgent two-hour session, to treat the manager of a well-known company in her office, and then home again for the rest! She was in terrible pain with her ankle and foot, due to an injury, and couldn't walk without crutches.

She also stressed on the phone the night before to me that she was exceedingly busy and would have to continue her work at her desk whilst I was treating her. What! Oh this is going to be great! I thought. Looking forward to this, I don't think! Having visions of me now, under her desk, suffocating with her foot in my hands, cramp in my legs and pain in my back, and for two hours? What if colleagues come in, how embarrassing is that?

Just one extra thing: Jo Jo, the daughter of Jacqui, a very good friend of mine, also rang the night before and said she desperately wanted a healing and could she have one tomorrow as she was going away the day after. I told her it was impossible as I was fully booked, starting with a trip to London. She had been diagnosed with cancer, and there was no way I wasn't going to fit her in somehow. I had been working on her with healing treatments each week for around a year at this point and was keen to keep them up.

"Oh, I have an idea," I said. "Do you fancy a couple of hours shopping in London tomorrow? If so, we could go up on the train together, and I could do healing on you for 40 minutes going up, go off to do my foot and ankle while you are shopping, and 40 minutes coming back. That would work, and I can put my hands on you discreetly whilst sitting in the train!" We both laughed and she agreed.

We settled ourselves in the train, and made sure we had a row to ourselves. I threw a scarf over her shoulder to cover my hand that was now placed on her stomach area. People were coming on and off the train, nobody noticed. As usual the passengers were in 'train daze mode', looking tired, bored, grey and blank!

We had only been going for about 10 minutes when I had this funny feeling. "Darling," I said, "something is not right." "What?" Jo Jo said, alarmed. "I have a feeling that the man sitting in front of me is not well," I replied. Our seats were facing forward, as was the person's in front of me, so we couldn't see him.

I got up quickly and moved to be able to face him. He was alone on this row. "Oh no! I think he is dying," I whispered. He was ashen and felt clammy. I asked him if he was OK. "No," was all I got out of him. Jo Jo and I looked at each other, and she saw where my eyes were going. "You're not, are you?" "Yup," I said, "I've always wanted to do this," and pulled the emergency handle to stop the train. That was a first!

The train came to a screeching halt, and I quickly thought I must help this man until the medics arrive, so I crouched down beside him and started healing him with my hand on his solar plexus. That was the best place, I thought, it will help him all over. Pandemonium in the train now – people shouting, pushing and trying to crowd in on us. The train security guard came rushing up to us and I said, "This man needs an ambulance now."

Of course, we had stopped dead in our tracks, excuse the pun! So the train started again with an announcement saying, "In five

A story of life-changing moments

minutes we will be in Twickenham. Everyone must disembark here. Please take the next train to Waterloo on platform 1. We apologise for any inconvenience."

Jo Jo and I stayed with the man, and gradually the colour in his face looked a bit healthier. I kept my hands on him until the paramedics arrived and then handed him over. The medics checked him over and said, "He needs to go to hospital immediately" The stretcher came in and he was taken off in the hands of the medics. And no, I never heard anything about our train man again!

The security guard said to us, "There is a train to Waterloo in 20 minutes, so you can catch that one." "Oh no," I said to him, "I am going to be late for an appointment for a VIP." "I tell you what," he said, "this train is going to Waterloo anyway, so don't tell anyone, just sit down and we will personally get you there as a thank you for helping that man." Our personal train! Wow, another first!

We were still chatting when we got out of the train, going over the events of the journey that we had just had. Jo Jo went off to do her shopping and I went off to do a foot!

I was quite tired when I got to the office, with spent-out adrenaline I think! Now I had to sit under a desk for two hours! I thought I would probably go to sleep if it was dark under there! I was not really looking forward to it. Well, it wasn't too bad. I was, in fact, on a chair at the side of her desk with her foot on my knee! She was on the computer some of the time, on the phone for a while, and then to my horror she had a staff meeting in her office with me still hanging on to her foot, for probably another hour. Well it felt like that!

Finally I left, and she felt better and the pain and swelling in her ankle and foot had reduced considerably. I was ushered out and on my way. I met up with Jo Jo and we giggled all the way home on the train with stories of the day. For me, this one was 'a last'!

Bravo! When I set eyes on Bravo, I fell in love with him straight away. We immediately bonded and he is my favourite of all the horses. We were actually not allowed to have favourites, or rather show we had, but for me he was an exception to the rule!

Nathalie and I had met through no coincidence! As one does! I was invited to a friend's amazing birthday party. It was a large do with tables set up for a formal dinner on a little island. A narrow footbridge led us there to enjoy the splendour of a candlelit dinner for around 30 people. The white table linen was adorned with candelabras in a setting so stunning, it could have been a scene from a period film or an Agatha Christie whodunnit!

I was sitting opposite a lovely and very engaging lady and we found ourselves chatting to each other most of the night. We both had lived in the Middle East and so were sharing our several 'matching' stories. Our conversation went on to horses. She said that her daughter had a few and was in dressage training with them and competing in national dressage shows.

I told her about my passion for horses and how I helped them in my work of 'horse whispering' and healing. She raised an eyebrow with an 'oh really' look and said, "You must meet Nathalie. She is picking me up later and I will introduce you to her. You would both get on really well."

It wasn't long after that evening that Nathalie rang me and asked if I could come over to the yard and treat a couple of her horses. "Absolutely, can't wait," I replied, and we fixed a day.

A story of life-changing moments

It was a beautiful, large, ranch-style property with a lot of land, outdoor arena and several stables. A rider's dream! She had a few horses at that time but the numbers have since increased to around 11 international and Olympic dressage horses.

When I was introduced to Bravo, that was it! It was love at first sight. I first go into the character and behaviour of a horse and find the areas that need help. Bravo was a loyal soul and a perfectionist when in the arena, he loved his work and particularly loved the music he danced to in the shows. He adored Nathalie and their bond was very strong.

However, he had a weakness in his back and an old injury in his back-right leg. So those were the areas I concentrated on. He absolutely loved the healing and felt everything that I was doing, knowing that I was helping him. I could see in his eyes the look of thanks for helping him and particularly the trust he had in me. We both felt that we had a strong connection to each other.

Then I went to the stable next to Bravo and met Pocket and started the same procedure with him. He was fairly new to the yard so Nathalie was anxious to know all about him, particularly his character, as he had joined the family with a clean bill of health and was totally sound.

He had quite a shy, nervous disposition and was very quiet and unsure of himself. I said this to Nathalie, but going further into his head, I turned round to her and said, "He is the jester of the yard, he likes to play tricks on you all and make you laugh." Nathalie thought that was a strange thing for me to say as she found him anything but that. "Well that is what I got, wait and see," I replied.

Several visits later, Nathalie, with excitement in her voice, told me about the pranks that Pocket had been playing: untying and pulling at boot laces, grabbing ends of zips on the grooms' clothing, throwing loose ropes up in the air, tipping buckets upside down, mouthing at hair toggles on anyone's hair that was near enough to get to, pulling strings on their tracksuit trousers, and more.

He was certainly 'the joker of the pack' and loved making people laugh. The other horses just looked at him with disdain when he did these things. However, all the humans laughed and he kept the yard in high spirits. Laughter is a healer on its own and that's what made it a happy yard. What more could you wish for?

It was quite a while later when Nathalie confided in me and said, "Do you know that when the first time you came here and gave me that information about Pocket being a jester, I was quite sceptical and I thought no, I don't think so." "Yup," I smiled. That happens with many, I thought to myself, quite normal! Nathalie continued, "But after seeing how he is now, you were so right and that made me make my decision that you were a 'must have' for this yard."

I went regularly to Nathalie's yard, either addressing a problem or simply maintenance 'top-ups'. After several visits and gaining the trust and love of all the horses, especially Bravo – whoops, shouldn't single him out – we all became a very bonded family.

One time, as usual, very early in the morning before their breakfast, I arrived, had a chat with them, waited until they finished their breakfast, then got started. Guess who was first? I went into Bravo's stable and did a quick scan around his body to see what I needed to address, then silently tucked into my work. Not long after I started, he became very sleepy, and decided to slowly buckle down on the ground. I laid down with him and stretched out alongside his relaxed body and continued my treatment. Gradually he put his sleepy head on my lap, shut his eyes, and was fast asleep in no time and snoring like a train. Bliss!

After that first time it used to happen again and again with, very often, a 'domino effect' of all the horses in the adjacent stables feeling the energy and going down to sleep until we had nearly a full stable of completely silent sleeping horses. Apart from the occasional snore from Bravo, of course!

Nathalie is an amazing person. Her horses are her passion. She is on a mission! With her love, which she gives in abundance to them, her determination, discipline, hard work and constant training, she will bring these horses into the Olympic arena, of that I have no doubt.

Over the years, Nathalie and I have become great friends and when I need a healing, guess where I go? Yes, to Bravo's stable for R&R and cuddles. He always gives back to me what I give to him. He is my healer!

Annie is one of my oldest and best friends. We first met when we were 18 years old in Scotland during the hunt ball season. Many years went past when we had lost touch and then I met her again during my flying days with BOAC. She was also a stewardess and latterly also married a pilot. We lost touch again for more years until Vicky, my daughter, and Annie's daughters were at boarding school together.

I was taking Vicky out for an exeat and she was bringing a friend with her so I had the two of them for the weekend at Moy Lodge. Soon I realised that Gemma was the daughter of Annie, my long-lost friend, and immediately we got in touch again and have been very good friends ever since.

As the years went by, and when I was in Singapore, Annie called me to say that Gemma's boyfriend had bone cancer. He had to have an operation to cut out the bone below his knee to his ankle, which was replaced with a titanium rod. Unfortunately, his body began to reject it and he acquired huge sores up and down the scar.

The surgeon was very disappointed and thought he would have to operate again and amputate his leg. With this news, I was horrified and decided to jump on a plane as soon as I could to get back to London and see if I could help him.

When I saw him, his leg was certainly in a mess. We chatted for a while and I kept saying to him, "Keep positive, just know that it will be fine." I put my hands on his leg and he said he felt an enormous amount of heat. I continued doing the same for as many days as I could before I had to return to Singapore. On my departure, I said that I would do distant healing on him every day. Not long after that, Annie rang me to say that the sores on Gemma's boyfriend's leg had disappeared and his body had accepted the titanium. His surgeon was extremely pleased and surprised as to the positive turnaround of his condition. to this day, he is enjoying life to the full with no further problems.

"It has been said that there is no such thing as coincidence in this world."

- Paulo Coehlo

CHAPTER 17

TWO PEOPLE AND A HORSE
Positive thinking and healing hands work miracles

Jen and I are very good friends and had been in Bahrain together for the 10 years we were there. Like me, she and her husband Suj are living back in the UK. We met up immediately when I returned and have been in constant touch ever since. From time to time, I would go and stay with them in Hitchin, to have quality time with them.

At that time, they lived in a large 'oldie worldie' rambling home with a beautiful entertaining garden. Suj had an antiques business, and his house was full of them and displayed all around. Here again, you could sense the energies from all around the world within his collection.

Both of them are great entertainers and they were frequently having parties. They had converted their cellar into an 'English pub' in which we spent many fun evenings with guests. Both of them were exceptional cooks and laid on feasts fit for a king, especially their Indian and Thai curries that were 'to die for'! When I stay with them, I always treat them to healings and aromatherapy treatments as thanks for their generous hospitality.

One day Suj rang me to say that Jen was not good. She had been to the doctor and was going through many checks, MRI scans etc. They found a malignant tumour at the back of her right eye, and she had to be operated on as soon as possible. The operation was due in a few days' time. Suj said, "Jen wants you with her, please can you come and stay during this time?" "No question of it," I said, "I am packing my bags now, and I will be with you as soon as I can."

Right, with 'collywobbles' of uncertainty and nerves running through me, with the thought of what Jen had to go through, I quickly rang to cancel appointments for the next few days, packed a case and jumped in the car.

On arrival, Jen, her usual positive bubbly self, told me what was going on with her and said she was keeping positive, and was so pleased I was with her. We put a plan in place for the next couple of days prior to the operation, of a timetable of healing treatments for each of them, and for Jen and I, quality time to be together, meditations, walks in the countryside, endless prayers and talks with the angels.

Jen had fasted the night before and now it was time to go into hospital. She was all dressed up, looking gorgeous as usual, with the last-minute addition of her favourite red hat!

When she is out and about, I don't think I have ever seen her without a matching hat! That's Jen! You would think we were going to the races rather than an admission to hospital. And that is how, within herself, Jen wanted to feel: dressed with confidence, courage, faith and positivity.

The three of us got in the car, with the feelings of fear of the unknown rising within our bodies, whilst on the outside we were joking, talking and helping each other to keep positive. We knew it was serious but we didn't voice it, or accept it.

A story of life-changing moments

So now we were in the private room and the nurses had got Jen into her bed, ready for the surgeon to come in. Soon he was beside us, and asked if I was family, if not would I please leave the room. Both Jen and Suj insisted I stayed as I was a very good friend and was like a part of the family, so I did.

The surgeon told us of the procedure that he would be doing and what aftercare would be done, etc. and then looked at Jen. "We do have to tell you that there may be a slight possibility that you could lose your eye, depending on the depth of the surgery, but we are hoping that it won't come to that, and we will of course do our very best to avoid that happening."

The words came as a shock and the three of us were speechless. We were silent for a while and trying to keep positive. We started chatting again, and all saying, "it will be fine," over and over. I said to her, "You won't lose your eye, I just know it!"

"Jen, I think we should start chanting the Eee Nu Rah invocation, to bring all the angels in with us and for them to come with you into the operating theatre, to be with you during the operation," I said. We were all up for this, but how about the staff?

Well, we will never forget it! I spoke to the nurses and said that this was what we wanted to do, and we would like to walk alongside her trolley until she reached the theatre. I said to them that it is a very powerful chant that brings all the angels in, and they could stay with her and look after her throughout the operation and give her healing for a quick recovery.

How they ever said yes, I will never know, but it was worth a try and the staff were great; they did believe in angels and if that is what would comfort Jen, yes, it was a go-ahead.

When Jen was wheeled to the operating theatre, Suj and I were by her side, and we were all chanting Eee Nu Rah, Eee Nu Rah, Eee Nu Rah Zay over and over till she disappeared through the theatre doors. Goodness knows what the onlookers thought, as we had some strange looks, but I am sure those that passed us benefited from the healing energies! OK, some of them may have thought we were from another planet! Actually, we were. We were within the planet of angels!

Suj and I left and went home and waited until she came out of theatre. When the phone rang to say she was coming out of the recovery ward soon, and all went well, we shot into the car and raced back.

When we arrived in her room, she was very sleepy and all bandaged around her head and right eye. The surgeon came in shortly afterwards and gave her the good news that her eye was intact, all went well. He was amazed that the recovery afterwards was so quick, and now she was chatting away in good spirits.

Along with the brilliant medical team and a little help from the angels, miracles happened! Jen was back to her usual happy self. Sometime after, she had a few corrective surgery procedures on her face and is now enjoying her life to the full. I often go to stay for a few days at a time to enjoy their company along with good wine and 'out of this world' curries.

I have to say, I often urge people to use the chant that we did if they are admitted to hospital for operations or any other procedure. It wasn't the last time I was to be present with others and repeated the same powerful chant!

Through Jen's contacts with many horsey people in her area, I now combine my stays with them to visit the yards, alongside Jen giving a helping hand, to administer treatments to a number of horses and owners. She is also a healer and uses many spiritual and alternative tools alongside conventional medicine.

Jen is one of the most courageous and positive people I have ever met. With her faith and outlook on life she has pushed through many barriers that others would find impossible. She now also encourages others to find their strength when they find themselves in a place of darkness, along with her amazing sense of humour.

Clare was given my telephone number by a friend of hers who I had been treating, along with her horses. She told Clare to get hold of me immediately as she had had amazing results from using me.

When I spoke with Clare on the phone, she was in such a terrible state of panic, and near to tears. I could hardly make out what she was saying. "Please come as soon as you can, Monty is in such a bad way, and the vets can't find out what is wrong with him. I don't know what to do and I can't stand seeing him going downhill so quickly." "Do you know what I do?" I said. "No," she replied, "but I have been on a search for someone like you." Ah, sceptical maybe but open, my last resort but worth a try, sounds about right – these were my thoughts at the time.

"Of course," I said, "where do you live?" "In Ledbury," she replied. Never heard of it. Probably in the middle of nowhere and where the sat nav doesn't pick up! A day out basically, by the time I got lost!

Although she gave me a quick résumé of the problems with her horse, it was so jumbled up with her emotions being all over the place, I really didn't get it all. I felt only the terrible feelings that she had, which were bringing her down, so I was eager to get there as soon as I could. We made a date for the following week, and she was able to calm down a bit before we put the phone down.

Oh OK, it's in Herefordshire I discovered when looking up the AA route finder on the computer. Knowing me, with my getting lost even with directions, I had better take a picnic in the car, just in case!

I set off early as I do for horses, at around 5am on a lovely sunny day with a picnic beside me. I thought it should be an OK drive with the beautiful countryside to enjoy along the way. Well, all was in good timing and I had half an hour left to arrive at the yard. I was now off the beaten track and going down little country lanes. Yes, you've got it, the sat nav failed! I stopped the car, now in the middle of nowhere.

When I parked up in a makeshift muddy layby, I rang her with hopes of the mobile connecting. It did. Whew! "You're not far away," she said, "go straight on, first left, cross over at the next junction, turn right down the first lane, then look out for the field full of hens on your right, pass them, and almost immediately there is a dirt track on the right, no signs, and then you are here. Should take you around 20 minutes." Wrong, 45 minutes later I arrived with my feathers all of a fluster!

Clare was overwhelmed to see me and flung her arms around me. She then took me straight to Monty's stable. I was shocked when I saw him. As he looked at me, his sad eyes were pleading for help. He was skin and bone, with muscle loss, and looked as if he could hardly keep himself upright. He shuffled and pivoted in stiff pain, very wobbly, head hanging down, and the energy around him was very low. It broke my heart to see such a forlorn creature in body, mind and spirit. We need a miracle here, I thought.

A story of life-changing moments

Clare told me what had happened. Monty had been struck down quite suddenly with a mysterious illness. He'd seen three vets and had been referred to have further tests. All were convinced cancer or something as sinister was underlying his chronic rapid muscle loss, but after every test under the sun and 12 days in equine veterinary hospital the vets were at a loss as to the root cause of the dramatic change to his once healthy and athletic body. He was like a body void of energy.

And that he was. When I put my hands on him it was like there was nothing there, no energy flow, feelings, or for that matter any problems! He felt like an empty body. Hard to describe as I had never had a case like this before. It felt that there was an imbalance everywhere, but it was like healing a carpet over skin and bones, with nothing underneath it. Like he had given up.

I voiced everything to Clare as I was going along. "Where is the problem?" she asked. "Everywhere," I said, "like a mind, body and spirit crash. But he'll be fine." She looked at me with belief, disbelief and hope in equal measure!

Yes, it was a mystery, and all the time, whilst the healing was channelling through my hands, I asked the angels for the miracle we needed. Whatever the cause, they would find it, and help him.

As my hands moved around his body, I could feel his energy gradually rising, and he was certainly accepting the treatment and absorbing every bit of it. He was very bonded with Clare, and they had been together forever, and he really wanted to pick himself up and be back to his old self.

We could actually see the dramatic transformation throughout the hour. His legs stabilised, his head came up, his eyes got brighter, his ears pricked up, and he became more alert and interested in his surroundings. He was now moving around easier and with much less pain.

Clare was so excited and moved about everything she had witnessed, and was over the moon and teary with the results. I told her he would get better and better and I would send him healing every day.

Before I left, I said, "I would like to treat you to some healing as I feel your stress, and this would help you. You also said you weren't sleeping well and this will do the trick." She was all but straight down on the stable floor to accept the much-needed offer. "Yes please," she said with gratitude in her tearful eyes.

The next day, Clare rang me to say thank you and said Monty was certainly different and the improvement was very noticeable. She said her sleep that night had been truly blissful.

We made another appointment, and when I arrived Clare said that Monty knew I was coming, which didn't surprise me! He had improved greatly and we saw more improvements through the second session. Clare was happy and calm now. She told me that when I first came, she thought she had a dead horse. Now look at him!

Sometime later, Clare sent me a video of Monty cantering around in the ménage. He was a free spirit again and back to his normal self. She was shouting for joy whilst filming it. I was near to tears. Thank you angels. The latest video I got from Clare was her, back in the saddle and riding her beautiful eventer, Monty. And what did the vets say? They were aghast at the total turnaround.

When Sue told me about her news, I was very concerned and said that I would do everything that I could to help her. She is the mother of Russ, my daughter's husband. We both get on very well and are very good friends.

She had a lump in her breast and the doctors told her that it was cancer and it had to be removed. She went into hospital and had the lump taken away along with some of her lymph glands. After that she had chemotherapy and radiotherapy.

Whenever I could, through all of the above, I was with her as much as possible. Sue lived in Angmering, about an hour and a quarter away from me, so I would get on the road early, between 5.30 and 6am, to be able to have a full day with her.

Each time I was with her we would do a healing session on the sofa in the sitting room. We would chat maybe during some of them, but mostly Sue would fall asleep. That is the best anyway, as with healing the body asks to be shut down so that the healing process can go deeper. This is why after having a healing you feel sleepier than normal in the early evening. It is then that the body is asking you to go to bed!

Sue loved the treatments, and said she could feel the heat, and thought it was a wonderful feeling. She described it as a warm glow working through her body and she could actually feel the healing taking place. She knew that she was going to be fine. Here again, we have one very positive lady!

Then we would chat endlessly about angels and how they were helping us. Bill, her husband, would pass in and out of the room with a sceptical look on his face and then a smile. Bill is a very practical and down to earth man, and angels were certainly not going to get into his belief system, yet!

When I threw in a fact about angels, he would say, "Right," and carry on walking! If I told him about one of the miracles I have witnessed, he would say, "Blimey," scratch his head and walk on!

It was time now for Sue's chemotherapy so off we went. This was the first time, and when we arrived, we thought what a ghastly depressing place. Thank goodness we were together. We needed some laughter in there!

As Sue was having her line put in, I said to her, "Don't forget the blue healing liquid visualisation." This I give everyone that is going through chemo, and as I have mentioned before, you visualise the chemo substance in the tube as a bright blue healing liquid, going through your veins and swirling around you inside. Visualise it going to the area which needs more help, and spend a little more time there. Just keep up the visualisation as much as you can.

At the same time, I would put a hand on Sue's solar plexus for deep healing. The rest of the time we would talk and laugh. Laughter helps you to heal! Please laugh! The state of the mind, as we know, is of the utmost importance. Keep positive and just know you will be fine.

Suddenly Sue was losing her hair and it was coming out in handfuls. She always dresses to perfection, very smart, colour coordinated with earrings, necklaces and other accessories to match. Now head turbans and scarfs had to be matched too, along with matching gloves.

This time when I was over, we decided to go and have a look at wigs. Sue had been given an address by the hospital for the specialist cancer wig makers. "I didn't know there was a difference, hair is hair isn't it?!" So off we went on a hair spree! We had a great laugh, both of us trying on ridiculous heads of hair, swapping about, and fooling around. I think we are meant to be serious in there!

It was amazing, Sue found a wig in almost her own colour and style. It looked stunning on her. "Did you ask the angels for that one?" I asked. "It is a pretty good replica isn't it? Well done."

Her fingernails also had all fallen off at the same time as her hair. It was pretty traumatic for her, to say the least. However, she never stopped smiling and never stopped herself looking anything but her best.

Every time I was with her, we would do healing treatments of course, meditations and visualisations, talk about the angels and use as many tools as we could think of for the healing to accelerate.

As I've mentioned before, the blue shower is a great visualisation tool that I give to everyone, especially cancer victims, so this was essential for Sue.

Every time you have a shower in the morning, visualise the water coming down, a bright sky blue colour, and instead of going over you, it is going inside your body. As it is coming down through your body, swirl this blue healing water a little longer in the areas that need more help. Then it flows all the way down till it comes to your feet.

As it goes out of your feet, visualise the colour turning brown and going into the drain, and right through the earth to be recycled. Visualise this procedure taking out all the toxins, sicknesses, diseases and negativity. Do this each day to rid yourself of any ailments. It is also important to do it every day to keep yourself healthy, even when symptoms have vanished.

This one is very powerful, and even if you forget to do any of the others, this one is a must. Many of my clients have been truly surprised and helped by this and have commented on the power of it. Just do it!

Sue and I continued to meet up whenever we could and work together with tools and the angels, until eventually after her journey of battling through terrible side effects, and medical intervention, she got the all clear. Her positivity throughout was outstanding, but of course she had the angels by her side, and we knew it.

We were all elated, and relieved that it was over, and she was on great form. Some days after the news, she told me that Bill, throughout the time we were working together, found so much support and strength from my presence. I was touched. Does he believe in angels now, I wonder?

Not long after that, to Sue's surprise, Bill came home with a little angel tattoo on his right shoulder, done with gratitude to the angels! Now he has his very own angel, and as Sue puts it, he now has Zoë and Sue sitting on each shoulder, looking after him!

"Ever felt an angel's breath in the gentle breeze? A teardrop in the falling rain? Hear a whisper amongst the rustle of leaves? Or been kissed by a lone snowflake? Nature is an angel's favorite hiding place."

- Carrie Latet

A story of life-changing moments

CHAPTER 18

FEAR AND UNDERSTANDING
Public speaking and an audience of horses

It was about a year after my divorce, when the pain of it had subsided, David and I decided to reconnect 'en famille', so we started having family Sunday lunches together. It is never the children's issue when marriages fall apart, and we felt it was very important that the children have their parents and grandparents in the harmony of a family unit.

It has worked extremely well, and from that, David and I are really good friends. He supports us all always, and we are a very bonded family. So now when we are all in the country, Sunday lunch altogether is always a priority. David has been for many years a speaker on cruise ships, with his subject being aviation. He is absolutely brilliant and brings humour to all of his talks. It was at one Sunday lunch that he suggested I should join his agency, so that I too could sail around the world, make a bit of a holiday out of it, with no expenses. So that is what I did, took the audition, got through, and prepared myself for my first cruise.

I was speaking to one of my best friends, Viv, on the phone, with a "Good morning darling, my guardian angel, good morning," that has been a forever start of our conversations, and we have a laugh about it each time. She is an amazing lady, like an angel indeed. Not a mean bone in her body, and helps everybody.

She has been a loyal friend and confidante throughout many years. Whenever I am struggling with things, or need to dump feelings of frustration, or just sharing, she is always there for me with words of wisdom. She has a great sense of humour and we always laugh through good and bad.

This time I was talking to her about going on my first cruise, and having to get eight talks together, could I do it, how would I get the time to prepare, off to Geneva for three weeks' work, loads of horses to do here, want to spend more time with the family, and so I rabbled on.

I thought, can I actually stand up and talk to around 3,000 people, plus being videoed at the same time to go through to the cabins? I know I am used to delivering talks and workshops, but being stuck with all these people on a ship and not being able to get away from them might just be too much to bare. What if I can't do it?

Words from Viv, in one sentence, "no pressure then darling, as usual you will work yourself ragged, multi-task to the dozen and I have no doubt that you will be brilliant, they will love you. You will be fine. Breathe!"

The day came quicker than I thought, and I was all packed, with a huge suitcase filled with multi changes for every occasion, of day wear, ball gowns, bikini, matching shoes, handbags and toiletries that weighed a ton. Not to mention the hand luggage of computer, reference books for my talks, and all my angels! I was now getting excited for the Mediterranean cruise of 10 days around Portugal with a couple of port stops. It was a Saga trip, so as you can imagine, I was probably the youngest on the ship!

A story of life-changing moments

Oh well, this will be easy, I thought, most of them will probably not hear my mistakes, or even the bulk of my talks! Could have a lot of questions afterwards though!

I was actually enjoying the cruise, but I knew I would enjoy it more when I got my first talk out of the way. I had prepared eight talks on alternative medicine, although I had been told when I got on board, I only needed to deliver five. I wasn't going to talk about angels this time as there would probably be a lot of sceptics in the audience, and apart from that, many of the passengers of a certain age looked as if they were not that far away from seeing them for real!

Here we go, in one hour I was due on stage. I was going over my talk on aromatherapy and I started to feel the nerves building up in my tummy, and I was pretty shaky before I even started. Whoops, better do some EFT on myself. Emotional Freedom Techniques was going to be my last talk. Maybe I should have done that first with the way I was feeling.

Public speaking is one of the top fears that people have, and EFT is probably one of the best things to do for getting rid of them. It works on the feelings that you have of old traumas and fears. If you get rid of that feeling, you can look at that trauma movie as if it wasn't yours, and will not be attached to it.

I have mentioned some of this before, that I use it on people and animals. I also advise everyone to look it up on the internet and learn about it, to be able to do it yourself. A must in my opinion, in everyone's tool box.

To explain it a little. If you imagine that your meridians are energy motorways and there is a car crash (trauma), you need to get rid of that block to clear the road. By tapping with different logarithms on your meridian points, it pushes that stuck feeling of the trauma out and the road is then cleared.

No longer will you have the feeling of that trauma, fear, or phobia. Obviously, you have to keep it up, with several sessions and then ongoing maintenance to work on general issues as well, but it is well worth it.

So there I was in my cabin, tapping away on the meridian points. The top of my head, along my cheekbone, under my nose, dip of my chin, breastbone, under my armpit, side of my hand, saying I'm fine, I am full of confidence, and now calming down a bit, at the same time looking at the clock to see how much time I have left.

The time went like lightning, and I felt I was not grounded yet. But time to go! Oh no, I thought, shall I fling myself overboard or just go with the flow? What flow! I felt my legs not walking properly as I shuffled down the corridors and made my way to the theatre. My laptop was slung over my shoulder, I was wildly tapping with my right hand on my head, collarbone, anywhere really and hoping that no one was looking and thinking that I had gone totally bonkers. Did I have time to be sick? No, I was there, dead on my allocated time for set-up.

Once I was on the stage, the mic fixed on to me, laptop set up, lights went on to a sea of faces, and I was introduced. First sentence is the worst, let's get that over! "Good morning ladies and gentlemen..." Amazing, I felt fine and rattled on in comfort with the whole talk. Good old EFT! It never fails!

After that, whilst meeting and chatting to the passengers and crew throughout the cruise, I had many people asking me for help and advice with ailments and pains. Did I ever say no? Of course not! The 'hands on deck' were mostly mine.

Horses and riders. What are the main problems with horses really? It may not be the past traumas, bad back, the saddles, injured legs and the food they eat, it could be the riders! As we

A story of life-changing moments

know, horses pick up whatever is going on emotionally with the owners, whether it be a bad relationship, bad mood, bad health, trouble at work, nervousness before an event, or just feeling under the weather and run down!

I had an idea: I was going to create an Angel Workshop for horses and riders. Simple really, it would be the same contents as with the humans but tailor-made to include the horses!

The first one I held was in Wales and I was really excited about this new venture. It was a new yard to me, and yes, it was in the middle of nowhere, so I had my usual routine of getting up early, getting lost, being there at a suitable time to be able to settle in, set up my venue for the humans and suss out the horses!

Sarah was a lovely lady, and she had an amazing yard. It was pristine clean, with an outdoor arena, a covered stable block of 10 stables with eight horses already in them, four on one side and the other four opposite. It was a livery yard, so there were many other horses going in and out of their stables from an additional block further away.

It was a bustle of the usual early morning duties, with sounds of buckets clanking whilst being filled with water, the sweeps of brooms in the stables, and wheelbarrows being pushed everywhere from the mucking out of the stables. The horses were being fed their breakfast bucket, and hay nets were put up, with almost immediately the sounds of munching from the hungry sleepy heads, in unison, around the yard.

Sarah pointed to the place where I would be starting with the humans, introduced me to the horses and their owners, then left me to wander around and set up my room. Right, I thought, I would set up the room first then quickly have a chat with the horses.

Having collected the workshop manuals from the car, eating my sandwich 'on the trot', I walked along the muddy path to the 'outhouse' where we would be working all morning. All I hoped for was that it would be warm in there! Hardy people the horsey lot, they didn't seem to mind the cold, rain or snow! For me it was the opposite, the hotter the better!

It was perfect, and lovely and warm. One big room, enough for eight people to move around in, leading through to a compact galley kitchen and loo. unusual to have a proper loo in yards, mostly they are little ones outside on their own, tucked away in places you can't find and jolly cold. Enough to make your eyes water, in fact most of them did, and you had to be quick!

I laid out the room with chairs in a semi-circle, manuals on chairs. Gave myself the comfiest chair opposite my participants, with a little table beside me with all my notes. Great, that was done, and then I went off to speak with the horses. The yard was buzzing now, with riders tacking up and trotting off to the arena, and others being led to the paddock. Little huddles of people having coffee, and beautiful sounds of the birds and the whinnies from the horses greeting their owners and other horses.

I went to each of the eight participant horses that were waiting in their stables for me, and had a quick chat with them all. For a short time, I scanned their bodies to see what we would be dealing with later, which gave me a head start. This area would be the venue for the afternoon, with the owners working on their own horses. Brilliant, I had found a collection of varied problems and emotions. It would be interesting to see how the riders and owners dealt with it. The energy was perfect, they all felt very comfortable with each other and that is what it is meant

A story of life-changing moments

to be like. No stress, calm. A good receptive group, I thought. Now it was time to 'rein in' my humans!

They were also a lovely group, seven females and one male, all of different ages and backgrounds. Perfect mix. Lovely energy between them. We did an introduction from each person and they stated what they wanted to get out of the day. All the same really – just getting to know their horse better and how to heal them.

"Well," I said, "the first and most important thing we need to do is get rid of any negative thoughts, emotions, anxieties, fears, old traumas, and day to day problems you have in your heads. It is important that you don't transfer these to your horses. Dump all your head problems in a bucket before you touch your horse! We all know that the horses pick up everything." Better use 'we' here, I thought, I don't want them to think I am looking or pointing a finger at anyone!

"All agreed, but easier said than done," they said! "You'll be fine," I replied. I told them the programme of the day, whereby the whole morning was for them, and then in the afternoon I would give them a demonstration of how to heal horses and after that they would be doing the same on their own horse. I started off by talking about the angels.

'What have angels got to do with it?' was the look on everyone's faces! 'Everything,' I thought. You all need extra help! So I told them how to talk with their angels and get their help.

Also, I told them that white feathers were presented to them by their angels, which is a sign that they are on the job of helping them with what they have asked for as well as mentioning other helpful tools, within the timescale I had. We then did chakra meditations to bring them into a peaceful state and clear their heads of negativity and their bodies of toxins.

I went on to explain, "now we are going to learn the basics of EFT, emotional Freedom technique, and we shall all do it. This will help you to clear whatever it is that you want to get rid of. Then when you get to your horse, you are empty of the stuff that shouldn't be sitting on his back and going into his head. You can also use this technique on your horse, which I will show you later."

When I explained how we do it, and what trauma or problem could be released, they all froze! Right, that's it, I thought, they are going to flee and gallop off into the sunset!

I told them this wasn't an in-therapy session, although I am a trained EFT practitioner; it was a short introduction of it and to give them a useful tool for them to use later, to help themselves and their horses. They can look it up on the internet and get the information on how and what it helps. Then if they really wanted to, they could find a practitioner if they felt they needed it. This is meant to be fun! But let's just feel it!

I told them that they needn't share their problems, each could just follow what I was doing and saying. We went into the basics and they were feeling the difference. They were astonished at what was happening to them, de-stressing gradually, and feeling good.

We were all very happy bunnies by lunchtime, and had our sandwiches and coffees near to the stables and chatted till it was time to go into the barn. Here we had one horse and its owner standing with me, with the audience watching. The connecting and healing began.

So, we had dumped all our stuff outside the barn, and had a calm clear head to begin on our horse. I talked them through what I was doing with my hands across his body. "Focus and feel. Feel where you feel there is a problem, don't guess or try to think too hard. You will just know. Don't question yourself. Your hands will get hot when you start healing, and just keep them there until you feel that it is finished."

"Move into his head, ask him questions, feel and hear the answers coming into your head, and listen. Don't struggle with trying to find them, they will come in naturally. Ask your angels for help, keep calm and don't think of anything, just wait. If you feel he needs tapping to help an issue, do it here," and I pointed below his ear, travelling across his cheekbone.

"Watch the horse's reactions, eyes closing off and on, large hippo yawns, resting hind legs in turn, or even going down to the floor to sleep. These are the signs that the healing is working." The horse that I was doing was giving all the signs that my group needed, bar him going down on the floor. Now they were ready to go and do their own horses.

It was a magical day, and all the riders and owners were in their stables with their own horse, talking to them, and healing them. I went from one stable to the next checking on each couple. There were a few things that I found earlier in the day with some of the horses that the riders didn't know about, and by the end of the day I was getting a confirmation of the new findings, from all of the riders and owners!

It was time to close, so I asked everyone to join hands in a circle between the horses' stables with the horses looking on in front and behind us. In a beautiful high energy that we could all feel, I asked them to close their eyes.

I took them into the chant of invoking the angels, "Eee Nu Rah." We did that for quite some time, feeling this amazing energy, the peace and silence around us. I was watching them all and the horses when I said softly, "Slowly open your eyes and look at your horses."

Every horse's head was turned towards us over the stable doors, with each one of them eyes closed and fast asleep! You could hear a pin drop. The silence was magical. It brought tears to everyone's eyes. Finally, before we parted, they all said they were 'blown away'. It's one of my favourite memories. No one will forget it. "So do you all believe in angels now?" I said with confidence. Affirmative from all!

"Angels are always with you. You're never alone, especially in your time of need. Listen in stillness for our guidance, which comes upon wings to your heart, mind, and body."

- Doreen Virtue

CHAPTER 19

MIRACLE BABY

There should always be hope so a light may shine

I met Zoë Smart a few years ago at Rony's clinic. She later made an appointment to see me. She was in a confused place in her life and asked me for help. She told me quite some time later that everything I told her was absolutely true, from where she was, how she felt, and where she was going, and then on to realising one of her biggest dreams. She was 'gobsmacked' she said, and has never forgotten that day.

Each time I was in Geneva, she would come and see me. Her life was well on track now, so it was just for general healings. She had a little girl already and now she was pregnant again. She was hoping to come and see me as I was soon to go out there, but a few days before my arrival she gave birth at 26 weeks to a little baby boy, Leo. He weighed a mere 1.9 lbs.

The first few hours and days for her were a blur as she was in complete shock. He was in the ICU and by day four the doctors told her that Leo needed to have an operation to treat his PDA (Patent Ductus Arteriosus). It was then, in despair, she went straight back to her hospital room and wrote me an email. She hoped I remembered her and was desperately asking for help, it was urgent.

I replied straight away and said I was sending healing and angels to Leo. Then I heard back from her saying the operation went well, but now the doctors were very worried that his intestines could become damaged. A plea for more help. My immediate reply was, 'Call me and I will give you some visualisation tools to use.'

She did just that, and we talked for a while and I gave her as many of the tools that I could think of to help her and Leo. Also, we talked about asking the help from our angels. I told her about the sign she would get to know that the angels were with her and helping. It would be a white feather.

Before we hung up, I told her I would continue every day to send healing and angels. Later she told me she was leaving the hospital that night, she met her partner and her daughter who were waiting outside for her, and as she looked down, she saw a white feather by her feet!

Two days after that operation, the doctors confirmed what they feared: Leo had necrotising enterocolitis, which had led to a perforation in his intestine. They needed to operate immediately.

Zoë called me again in a terrible state, saying this was such a big operation and she just hoped he would survive. "Keep positive," I said, "and I will be flying over tomorrow and will ring you as soon as I get there."

The flight seemed endless, and I was just praying that Leo would be OK. The thoughts of what Zoë was going through were unimaginable. A mother's worst nightmare.

I rang Zoë as soon as I landed, and found out Leo got through the operation and was fighting for his life. I asked if I could come and see him tomorrow, Saturday, if of course the staff

A story of life-changing moments

would let me into the ICU. No way were they going to let me into the Intensive Care unit, but it was worth a try!

Zoë said to the nurse that she wanted a healer to come in and spend some time with Leo, and so the nurse asked the doctor. His reply was, "Any help would be good in this case, so yes, on the condition that she doesn't set their machines off!"

When I arrived at the hospital and met Zoë, she looked worn out and anxious, but was so thrilled to see me. We hugged each other then went up to the ICU. I was given a mask and gloves and in we went. It was heart-wrenching to see these little babies on support machines and fighting for their lives.

It was silent in the room, bar a couple of nurses moving from one baby to the other, checking monitors, adjusting tubes, and changing dressings. I was led to Leo's incubator and it broke my heart to see this tiny little thing fast asleep, with tubes attached to him, and trying desperately to survive.

Well, now what, I thought, do I put my hands through the port doors of the incubator, obviously I can't touch him, or do the healing from the outside? Zoë interrupted my thoughts by opening the little port doors, and said, "There you go!"

Gently, I put my hands through and kept them a couple of inches away from his body. Zoë said she would leave me with him on my own and would come back in an hour.

"OK fine," I said. Any minute now, I was expecting doctors or nurses to charge up to me and say, "What do you think you are doing? Get your hands out of there immediately." However, as the staff came in and out in silence, no one spoke to me, came near me, or uttered a word! Obviously, the staff had been primed by the doctor to leave me in peace!

Zoë came in when I had finished, then we left, de-gloved, de-masked and went downstairs. Then she said to me with a worried look, and I already knew what was coming, "Will he survive?" Immediately, I replied without any thought, "He is an old soul, very strong, and of course he will." I just knew it.

Before I left, I gave her my angel stone, which I charged with healing energy specifically for Leo. From that day on it was always in the incubator with him. By Monday Leo still hadn't had any bowel movements, so again Zoë asked me for help. Straight away, I said, "Poo angels on their way!" Later that day she picked Leo up for his daily cuddle and kept the angel stone in the hand that was covering him. When the nurse picked him up to put him back in his incubator his little stoma bag was full of meconium.

I started work at the clinic on the Monday, but was in touch with Zoë every day about Leo's progress. By Wednesday, the doctors considered he was doing so well that he could be moved to the neonatal unit, and on the Friday, he was taken to his new home.

Saturday morning, I was back to see Leo and give him his usual hour's healing. When I went into the neonatal unit with Zoë, and started to open the port doors of the incubator, the new nurse that was looking after him was furious and forbade me to put my hands in. "OK no problem, I shall place them outside the incubator," I said. She said that she found my visit 'destabilising' for Leo. By request of the mother, I carried on regardless.

When Zoë returned that afternoon, the same grumpy nurse was very excited! She said that Leo had had his best day yet, and they had turned the CO_2 in his oxygen down to 32%! A couple of days later, Zoë went down to the hospital to find Leo clutching his angel in his tiny hand!

A story of life-changing moments

When I returned to the UK we kept in touch, promising to send Leo and the family distant healing every day. The doctors apparently constantly expressed surprise at Leo's recovery and progress. Three months later he had an MRI of his brain and the doctor who did the reading of the scan could not believe it when she was told how premature he had been.

Not long after, Leo had a scheduled stoma reversal operation. The surgeons told the family that recovery could take anything from a few weeks to many months. He would have to be fed through a tube until he could again drink breast or bottled milk.

Zoë and I were in constant touch over that time. Not only did the operation go very well but the surgeons were astounded to see that within a couple of days he was drinking again from a bottle and having bowel movements.

Within less than a week he was ready to be discharged but unfortunately caught a bacterial infection. This sent Zoë over the edge, and she rang me in hysterics, saying that she felt Leo and she couldn't take any more, they had been through so much, etc. I tried to calm her down and reassured her he would be fine.

Four months from his birth, Leo finally went home. Four months later he had his first big evaluation in terms of development. He passed all his tests with flying colours. The last time I was in Geneva, Zoë, Leo and I had lunch together. It was a magical reunion. He came straight into my arms, put his head on my shoulder, and almost immediately fell asleep.

"The most incredible thing about miracles is that they happen." –

- *G K Chesterton*

Chapter 20

HORSE WHISPERING
Healing through words and touch

During one of the times I was in Dubai, Maggie, who makes appointments for me and organises my schedules and animal visits, said, "Dubai Eye, the radio programme, want to interview you whilst healing a horse. I have a horse for you to do anyway tomorrow, so I will ask the owner's permission to use hers for the programme." "Oh OK," I said. Maggie made the call and our request was granted.

Great! It is always fine when I am doing the healing with the owner alone, to get him or her with my full attention, but with possibly an audience, people chatting, a microphone, and ambience of several energies, this could be difficult!

So off we went to a yard in the middle of the desert somewhere, and thank goodness I wasn't driving, otherwise we would have landed in Abu Dhabi. Maggie took us straight there with her calm high efficiency, as usual, and we arrived early. Brilliant, I can suss the place out!

It wasn't that long before the owner arrived, and almost at the same time Suzanne appeared, carrying camera, microphone and notepad. Suzanne asked if she could speak to me on her own to start with, and we duly sat down on a bench in the yard, away from the stables.

Ah, notebook first, I thought, as she scribbled away getting some of my background: how I got into horses, cats, dogs and other species, including humans! "Which are the easier to do?" she said. "Animals," I replied, "they don't talk back, listen to everything I say, accept, trust, and allow the healing to happen."

She then recorded an in-depth interview of questions about horses, and the procedure of healing. This would also include the session in the stable, of explaining everything that I was doing, and found on the horse.

Before we left to go to the stable, I condensed my intentions. "I will find out what is going on in his head, if he wants to tell me something, find out any anxieties there, go around his body with my hands to see where he needs help, then do the healing on the areas that need it, basically. I never know what's going to happen 'til I get there, so let's just go with the flow and see what happens." All said quickly in almost one sentence and one breath!

When we got to the stable, oh no, there were quite a lot of inquisitive humans lurking around, I hoped they were not going to crowd in and crash the energies around me and my patient!

So I was standing beside my horse, actually it was a pony, in the stable, after saying to the onlookers, "Please keep a distance from the stable door, as I don't want to be working with mixed energies here, thank you." And they all politely stepped back.

Suzanne was in the stable with me and near enough for my voice to be picked up on the mic. She was lovely, a quiet voice whilst she was asking me some, but not too many, questions, camera shots done discreetly, and microphone slowly pointing

A story of life-changing moments

near to me, luckily black and not orange, so no chance of being mistaken for a carrot!

I went into the pony's head first, and told the owner and the audience how she was a bit distrustful of me, but she would gain confidence as I go on. I did some EFT tapping on her head, found out about some things that she didn't like, particularly loud noises and swift movements.

She was a 15-year-old ex-polo pony, and had been pushed too hard by her previous owner, which I found out from the pony, but now she was very bonded and happy with this owner of two years. I did my usual scan around her body, then concentrated on the tendon injury she had on her hind leg. After that I did a general re-balancing. The owner confirmed my findings.

Chatting was going on outside the stable door. Typical! I was worried the horse would not get the best out of my healing!

Suddenly, she gave huge hippo yawns. Now we definitely had her trust and acceptance. Her chin wobbling, resting a back leg, and, my goodness, she was getting down on the ground to go to sleep! She thoroughly enjoyed her healing, even in front of camera, mic, and inquisitive humans! If only horses could talk!

When it came out on the radio, my interview started and ended with that lovely song 'Talk to the Animals' from Doctor Doolittle. Straight from the horse's mouth!

"Your angels are listening.
Talk to them and ask for their help."

www.theartofancientwisdom.com

FINALE

The time has flashed by and my children and grandchildren are speeding ahead in years. Charles has two boys, Harry 14 years and Matthew 12 years, and Vicky has Toby who is 7 years and Hannah, our little girl, who is 2 years old, all of whom are amazing, beautiful souls. Family is the most important thing in our lives, and the joy we get from them is unsurpassable. We all have a strong bonding of unconditional love.

I know what you are going to say! Do my children and grandchildren have my gifts? Yes of course they do. Both my children, of whom I am very proud, have succeeded in working on their mission.

Charles has now been working with the NHS for over 15 years. His mission is helping people as a paramedic, starting from working in the ambulances, to first response on motor bikes, and then on to helicopters with the trauma doctors. He is certainly hands on and has saved many lives. He hasn't a mean bone in his body and would help anyone. He has the most amazing bedside manner whilst dealing with patients, which reminds me of my father. He is a healer for sure.

Vicky has her own business in marketing. She has an amazing strength of character and has achieved all the goals she has set herself. The way she handles people is incredible, she is a one off, and an old soul. Her gift of helping and handling people, with her wisdom and right words at the right time, is remarkable. Her natural counselling skills are invaluable for anyone that needs help. She also hasn't a mean bone in her body.

Yes, all my grandchildren are very intuitive, can heal and see angels! They have me as a grandmother, don't forget! They have all spent hundreds of hours with me, cuddled up in my four-poster bed, doing hands-on healing for aches and pains and talking to the angels. What did you expect?!

In my life there is a pecking order: family first, my mission of healing and helping people second! Oh, the other thing that I often say to my children, "There are two things I don't like to share: one is my grandchildren and the other, chocolate!" I seem to have a bit of a reputation for that.

All through my life I have pushed through the barriers of what I thought I couldn't do and did it anyway. When I listened to my inner self and didn't take heed of the messages, I made mistakes. From them, I learnt more and gathered more strength for the next challenge. You have to try, fail and try again. Never give up.

I knew from the beginning of my life I was here to heal. Although then I knew it, but didn't know I knew it! As years went by it was made evident and I naturally progressed by being led from all the non-coincidences!

We are all healers and you can do it too. Just feel it, with thoughts of intention, and just know that it works. Ask your

A story of life-changing moments

angels to help you. Do it often and you will be surprised with the results.

For yourself, for your health, both body and mind, visualisation tools are powerful as I have said before, so try and fit them into your daily routine. In addition, it is essential for you to be in nature, where you receive the universal energies. Go walking by water, into the woods, open spaces, up mountains, to get your happy pills. This is powerful medicine and a gift of nature.

If you feel depressed, throw yourself out there, do a bit of EFT Tapping at the same time, and you will soon feel the difference as your spirits gradually heighten. As you probably know by now, your guardian angel and other angels are always with you. You are never alone. talk to them and keep them in your life, to help, guide and comfort you.

The words of wisdom from my parents took me through my life. My husband gave me encouragement to continue on my mission. My children have taught me many valuable lessons through their years, and my grandchildren show me every day the magic of pure love. My twin sister always travels within me, and shares, either by my side or at a distance.

The many experiences I have had in my life and the people I have touched have been overwhelming and I have always been there for everyone when at all possible!

It is so satisfying to be able to help make a difference to someone's life, be it human or animal, to heal or to help. It's not me, remember, that performs miracles. I am just the vehicle for the higher energies to work through me. I have helped/healed so many people over the years. Most have come on their own volition. Others would never themselves have considered healing and have been brought to me by friends or family.

One of the people who, by his own admission, was not a believer until he met me, was John. He wanted to fight his cancer from every angle, and so visited me alongside receiving standard medical treatment.

When I realised that his own affirmation was, "It'll be fine" – so similar to Mummy's that I heard so often growing up – I felt a real connection. John's advice to others, "embrace healing... believe, believe, believe some more."

I am very much a 'hands on' person, in every meaning of those words. My children and grandchildren are definitely 'hands on' and to my friends and clients I do extend a hand or two!

The most important thing to me in my life is my family, with the unconditional love that we have for each other. Life is love, and love is all there is.

I embrace life, and live it to the full. I hate missing out! So it's early to rise, with the burning of candles, very often into the early hours!

I am still continuing my work in Geneva, Dubai and the UK and will go anywhere in the world where I am needed, if I can.

Will I ever retire? nope, Hands On Forever.

"Twenty years from now you will be more disappointed by the things you didn't do than by the ones you did do. So throw off the bowlines. Sail away from the safe harbor. Catch the trade winds in your sails. Explore. Dream. Discover."

- Mark Twain

ABOUT THE AUTHOR

ZOË HENDERSON

Zoë is a captivating presence. Her enormous energy together with her complete commitment to helping all those in need are her divine qualities.

She tirelessly uses her abilities to improve the lives of humans and animals alike. She never stands still and constantly looks for new ways to communicate the powers of the universe, whether to an individual or by speaking in front of an audience or hosting an Angel Workshop in any part of the world.

These days, her international reputation takes her to Switzerland where she holds clinics in French and to Dubai where she has a long waiting list. She returns to both places three or four times a year for two to three weeks, administering her healing to all ages and creeds and, of course, to animals, especially horses with whom she has a very special communication. She says that many psychological problems with an animal can emanate from the handler, so any healing has to be for both of them.

In England, Zoë spends as much time as possible with her family. She has two children and four grandchildren from ages two to 14, all of whom have spent many hours in her playful company and share her easy relationship with angels and other energies through her teachings, of course.

Although her family comes first, Zoë does have clients in the UK and is often up before dawn to drive to stables in the West Country to treat her equine fraternity there or to visit someone who is incapacitated and can't come to her. In any spare time, she keeps up with her close friends who also benefit from her knowledge and abilities and happy disposition.

She says her vitality and power have increased with her years and that she has an irrepressible desire to use them to the utmost to heal and to teach others how to find or improve the positive aspects of their lives through the help of the universe as she knows it.

Zoë has also been painting from childhood, later at art college, and then has continued throughout her life. Her 3D paintings are channelled, and she creates them with sculptured silk on canvas, then painted over in oils – often personalised to individual choice. She has had exhibitions in Scotland, England and Geneva.

www.intuitivehealer-horsewhisperer.com

Printed in Great Britain
by Amazon

77789480R00120